PROJECT RECOVERY

Playbook for Project Janitors

How Quiet Leaders Take Over, Clean Up, and Lead

D. CIARCIA JR., PMP, PJ

PROJECT RECOVERY

Playbook for Project Janitors

How Quiet Leaders Take Over, Clean Up, and Lead

KIMBER BOOKS

D. Ciarcia Jr., PMP, PJ

KIMBER BOOKS PUBLISHING GROUP
U.S.A.

A Kimber Books publication / published by arrangement with the author

This book blends professional experience, historical events, and fictional parables. The fables and illustrative stories are the author's creations, intended as teaching tools. References to historical projects, organizations, and public events are drawn from the public record but retold for context and learning. Any resemblance of fictional characters to actual persons, living or dead, is coincidental. The perspectives and lessons offered reflect the author's own experiences and interpretations.

PLAYBOOK FOR PROJECT JANITORS:
HOW QUIET LEADERS TAKE OVER, CLEAN UP, AND LEAD
Copyright © 2025 by D. Ciarcia Jr.
Cover art © 2025 Kimber Books / kimberbooks.com
ALL RIGHTS RESERVED

PRINTED IN THE UNITED STATES OF AMERICA

No part of this book may be copied, scanned, reproduced or otherwise distributed in any form without permission. Please do not encourage or condone the illegal use of copyrighted material in violation of the author's rights under law.

ISBN-10: 1-969068-00-0
ISBN-13: 978-1-969068-00-3

Dedication

To the ones who came before me,
who taught me that service is not weakness,
that care is not naïve,
and that leadership can be as quiet as a mop passed from
one hand to the next.

To every mentor, teammate, and client who let me walk
beside them, even when the path was cluttered, uncertain,
or thankless.

And most of all, to you, the reader who chose to pick up
this book, willing to carry the keyring, the broom, the
weight, and the work.

May you find, as I did, that the deepest rewards of a career
are not in the spotlight, but in the trust left standing when
the lights go out.

-- D. Ciarcia Jr., PJ

D. Ciarcia Jr., PMP, PJ

PLAYBOOK FOR PROJECT JANITORS

Chapters

Preface - Inheriting My First Mess: The Mound	9
Chapter 1 - Welcome to the Cleanup Crew: Embracing the Role of Project Janitor	12
Chapter 2 - Brushing Away Ambiguity: Defining the Scope of the Mess	21
Chapter 3 - Sweeping With Purpose: Building a Clear Vision	30
Chapter 4 - Spinning Expectations: Shaping Stakeholder Priorities with Precision	40
Chapter 5 - Custodians of Communication: Clearing the Pipes	49
Chapter 6 - Stocking the Closet: Resources and Tools to Tackle Disorder	60
Chapter 7 - The Overflowing Bucket: Managing Risks and Spills	70
Chapter 8 - The Janitor's Crew: Building Trust to Lead Your Team Forward	78
Chapter 9 - Mopping Up Missed Minutes: Managing Time and Deadlines	87
Chapter 10 - Holding the Janitor's Keys: Navigating Accountability and Authority	96
Chapter 11 - Unclogging the Drain: Staying Grounded While Monitoring Progress	105
Chapter 12 - Inspecting the Corners: Ensuring Quality Under Pressure	114
Chapter 13 - Recovering a Slippery Start: Containing the Spill and Owning the Origins	123
Chapter 14 - Buffing Away Resistance: Change That Holds Without Force	132
Chapter 15 - Polishing the Tarnish: Revealing the Treasure Hidden in Chaos	141
Chapter 16 - Ready for Inspection: Testing, Training, and Transition	150
Chapter 17 - The Point of the Cleanup: Closing the Project with Confidence	158
Chapter 18 - What We Missed: The Project Janitor's Hardest Lesson	167
Chapter 19 - The Janitor's Inspection: Holding the Line After the Calm	175
Author's Epilog - The Project Janitor's Final Sweep	186

Preface
Inheriting My First Mess: The Mound

It began with a mound. A waterlogged pile of clay-laced earth dumped unceremoniously in the corner of the schoolyard. It sat there in silhouette, blocking the view of the farmer's house beyond the fence, daring someone to care.

I was in sixth grade. Not chosen. Not destined. Just present. The one who had been chosen, some older boy with louder confidence, had stepped away mid-promise. A few shovel strokes, no glory found, and he was gone. The dirt remained. Unleveled. Untamed.

And then there was Mr. Planwell. He bore the title Janitor, a word the world now resists but one he wore with proud, quiet dignity. Tall and slope-shouldered, with hands calloused from repairs no one saw him perform, he moved through the school like it was a place he'd earned, not just worked. He spoke sparingly, but each word had weight and those around him noticed. The air around him always carried the faint scent of a working utility sink, mop heads soaking in ammonia. Not unpleasant. Just honest. Like someone who had already cleaned up more than you'd ever know.

Each afternoon, waiting for the late bus, I followed him. Sometimes with a broom. Sometimes with a bucket. Sometimes with nothing but a question I didn't yet know how to ask. One day, he walked me out to the mound. Said nothing at first. Then: "I need someone who finishes what others don't. You up for that?" He didn't call it leadership. He didn't call it service. He called it done. Somehow, that was heavier than all the rest.

I looked at the mess. Jagged, half-covered with new spring growth and streaks of stubborn, melting snow. I felt the pause. There is a part in every story where a child misses the sign or picks up the shovel. Unsure, I took the step. Not from confidence, but from the echo of his voice felt down to my toes.

He laid out the vision: a baseball field. Bases aligned with geometry's grace. Mound measured, set to just the right height. Grass trimmed to meet expectation. The chain-link fence stood waiting. Rusted in spots but steady. My project kickoff was to weave meaning through it, one plastic slat at a time, until it looked less like a barrier and more like a homerun dare. Spring had arrived, and the field needed to be ready before the schoolyard filled again.

At first, we were a legion. Shovels in hand. Dreams held tightly like task lists in our pockets. Friends gathered not for fame but for the breath of shared purpose. We dug. We raked. We shaped. We laughed too, because laughter, like sweat, marks progress. The scent of turf and youth mixed with whatever clung to my shirt from the supply closet, bleach maybe, or pine cleaner, the kind that lingered on mops long after they were rehung on the janitor's closet wall.

Then April rained. And rained again. The clay turned to sludge. The pile rejected our intentions. Wheels stuck. Boots sank. Spirits followed. The crowd thinned. I began to understand abandonment, not as malice, but as weather.

Still, Mr. Planwell never looked disappointed. He never reminded me who had failed before or that failure was even possible. He'd hand me another tool, as if to say: Keep trying.

So, I did. I recruited younger kids with wide eyes and no sense of scale. They brought energy, if not endurance. We worked when the sky allowed. Sometimes past sunset under the warm hum of streetlamps. Sometimes alone, creating order from chaos. Sometimes with grownups after Sunday church, ties loosened, sleeves rolled up, stories shared in the long light of memory.

The field began to form. Not all at once, but in whispered arrivals. First came the shape. Then the chalk lines. Then came the understanding that vision lives in returning, refining, and showing up, with a good plan, willing hands, and quiet courage, again and again.

When it was finished, it didn't shine. It glowed. The reddish brown of the infield swept clean and steady beside the green. Each base a milestone. The fence, the line we reached and didn't step past.

On the last day of summer, we played. First at-bat went to me. Not because I deserved it, but because I stayed. The crack of the bat was more than wood meeting ball. It was closure. It was proof. My foot touched first base, and for a moment, the grounds paused to nod.

That field never made the news. It didn't last forever. But it imprinted something that did, for me.

Because that mound, that first mess, was more than a project. It was a metaphor. A parable. A whisper from the future saying:

This is what you'll do. You'll be called in late to someone else's failure. You'll see the mess and still begin. You'll work with borrowed hands, uneven plans, fading light. And still, you'll build the field.

You will build the field.

That is the heart of a project janitor. We do not build from blueprints alone. We build from belief. From tenacity. And sometimes, when the work is good enough, we get to take the first swing.

Thank you, Mr. Parker, -er, I mean Mr. Planwell. Behind every lesson worth carrying forward, there was someone real who lived it first.
-- D. Ciarcia Jr., PJ (Project Janitor)

Project Janitor *noun*
/ˈprä-jekt ˈja-nə-tər/
1. A project leader who is brought in midstream to stabilize, recover, and complete troubled initiatives.
2. An experienced professional who restores clarity, scope, and accountability in projects derailed by drift, poor oversight, or misaligned execution.
Usage: Unlike traditional project leaders, project janitors are tasked with cleanup, course correction, and making the work hold quietly and without fanfare.

Note: If you've ever salvaged a Sunday dinner, a system integration, or a skyscraper, you're a project janitor. The scale doesn't matter. The instinct does.

Chapter 1
Welcome to the Cleanup Crew: Embracing the Role of Project Janitor

Executive Summary

Mid-project recoveries rarely begin with clarity. Leadership injects a new project leader with little warning. Someone who inherits the mess and the expectation to restore project direction and momentum. Daunting. This book reframes this challenge through the lens of the "project janitor," a project leader who is brought in midstream to stabilize, recover, and complete troubled initiatives. Someone who listens before acting, repairs what others overlook, and restores function without fanfare. Through metaphor and example, this chapter outlines how presence, pattern recognition, documentation, and calm discipline form the foundation of effective recovery. When handled well, your work leaves no footprint, only progress. But without context, even the best cleanups fail. The key is to notice what others step over, and to act without waiting to be handed the mop. Ready to fill the bucket?

The Mess at Hand

It doesn't begin with a kickoff meeting or a clean slate. It begins when you step into a space someone else has already occupied, half-built and fraying at the edges. There are notes taped to the wall, faded timelines on whiteboards, coffee rings on a stack of old printouts that no one bothered to throw away. The project is already in motion, somewhat, and you are not the architect or the originator. You are the one called in after the drift, when progress stalls and patience thins. The one handed a task no one wants to name but everyone needs resolved. Not a rescuer. Not a hero. A cleaner of corners, a gatherer of threads. A project janitor.

The work is not glorious, though it is sustaining. You arrive after the damage has already been done. After deadlines have slipped. After trust has eroded. After meetings have filled with nods and empty agreement. The trace of burnout still lingers, even if the team smiles politely when you enter the room. You inherit a project that has wandered off its map, if there ever was one. People expect you to find the path forward, but first you must figure out where you're even standing. That moment, where clarity hasn't yet arrived, but accountability has, is where the real work begins.

You begin not with answers, but with attention. Before solutions can take shape, you must absorb the environment, its tensions, its tempo, its unspoken rules. Listen in meetings where no one speaks plainly. Read the notes no one intended you to find. Walk the halls, digital or real, with your senses attuned to the places people avoid mentioning. The mess may be well evident, but it is rarely loud. Leadership wants it swept into the corner. That mess resides in silence, in deferment, in the faint pause after someone says, "We've always done it that way." Your first responsibility isn't to fix. It's to understand.

Every inherited project carries a shadow history. What's broken isn't always visible in the code or the charts. It lives in the decisions that were never documented, the debates that ended without resolution, the emails never followed up. You are not only managing tasks; you are managing ghosts. Each missed deadline or vague requirement is a symptom of something earlier, a slippery moment where someone chose speed over clarity, silence over conflict, or pride over partnership. Part of your role is to reconstruct that history, not to assign blame, but to understand how the present came to be. Armed with the tales that lost the timeline, all that matters now is what you do next. Remember that, always.

Begin with orientation, not acceleration. The instinct will be to fix, to build charts, to hold meetings that reclaim control. But you cannot restore what you do not understand, and you cannot lead what you have not yet joined. Take time to see the people behind the tasks. Their silences. Their shorthand. Their plans long buried, still echoing in how they speak and what they say. The heart of a matter speaks before the voice knows how, and through that voice, the truth begins to surface. Every sigh holds a story. Every shortcut has a reason. If you move too quickly, you'll miss the clues. If you listen well enough, the next step will often announce itself.

The Cleaning Strategy

Patterns will begin to emerge. Not in bold outlines, but in subtle recurrences like missed handoffs, repeated delays, moments where meetings dissolve without decisions. These are not isolated incidents; they're signatures of something deeper. Resist the urge to label too quickly. Instead, watch how the same confusion reappears in different forms. Follow the loops, not to assign fault, but to trace design. Because every mess, no matter how sprawling, has a shape. And within that shape lies your map forward.

Before a project janitor can restore direction, they must rebuild alignment. Not the ceremonial kind that lives in mission statements, but the practical kind that shows up in calendars, code branches, punch lists, and elevator conversations. People must begin to move in rhythm again, even if the melody has changed. You don't impose that cadence. You invite it by modeling clarity, by repeating what matters, by noticing when things begin to hum. Most of the time, alignment doesn't arrive with a declaration. It returns like trust does, in the repetition of honest work.

Once the rhythm begins to return, even faintly, you can begin to reintroduce purpose. Not by handing out vision decks or rallying cries, but by naming what's already moving and why it matters. Purpose is fragile in the aftermath of burnout. It must be rebuilt slowly, through relevance, not rhetoric. Show how the work connects, how the effort accumulates. Let meaning emerge from motion, not mandate. If your team can see the shape of progress, they will begin to believe in the direction again, even if no one's said the word "vision" out loud. Consider this time to be the pied piper, not the visionary in an ivory tower.

Scrub Away the Chaos

Your role now is to protect that fragile return. Not by tightening control, but by balancing clarity with compassion. A recovering team still needs a roadmap, just not the kind used to justify pressure or assign blame. They need direction without judgment, structure without suffocation. Let people find their footing within the framework you build. Celebrate progress without demanding perfection. Never demand perfection. Both perfection and perpetual motion are myths. This is a time to steward momentum, not own it. If you hold the reins too tightly, you risk choking the very trust that began to grow. Sometimes leadership means stepping back just enough for others to step forward.

PLAYBOOK FOR PROJECT JANITORS

There will be days when managing the cleanup crew feels thankless. When your late nights and subtle nudges go unnoticed. Your guidance misinterpreted. Your presence mistaken for control. You may inherit resentment meant for someone who came before you. Or for no one in particular. That, too, is part of the cleanup. You are absorbing more than risk; you are absorbing weight. Emotional sediment from months of confusion, fatigue, and failure. It is not your job to carry it all, but it is your job to notice it, name it, and never add to it. A project janitor carries accountability, often without authority. Carry it well.

Progress will not always feel like progress. Some weeks, it will look like fewer dropped handoffs. Fewer panicked emails. A meeting that ends on time with no one raising their voice. These are not victories that make headlines, but they mark the slow return of operational trust. You are not here to announce momentum. You are here to recognize it. See it when it flickers, when it steadies, when it begins to move under its own weight. This kind of progress won't be written into the corporate structure. But it settles into the foundation. It lasts.

Don't expect recognition. That may come, but don't expect it. The nature of your role is to clean up without drawing attention to the mess. If things go well, others may believe the turnaround happened on its own. That's fine. Let them. Visibility is not the measure of value. What matters is that your presence shifted the arc. That which was unraveling, now holds. What was chaotic now breathes. You're not the story. You're the reason it can continue. Make the project boring. Keep it under the radar. Now, that's a true sign of project janitorial success. Embrace it.

No one will tell you it's time. There's no signal, no ceremony, just a moment when the silence no longer pushes back. You'll notice a pause after your questions. A teammate asking for clarification instead of nodding along. The space between issues and excuses starts to shrink. That's when you act. You rewrite the meeting agenda to reflect reality instead of ritual. You revive the RAID log and start using it, live, in front of the team. You name risks. Confront assumptions. You call out dependencies before they blindside delivery, again. These aren't dramatic moves, but they matter. You're not asking for permission to lead. You just lead. You remove friction where it slows the work. Bit by bit, the team starts to notice, not because you're louder, but because things move more easily around you.

You no longer need to initiate every move. Instead, you begin to spot signs of shared ownership taking hold. Someone updates resources and percent completes in the project schedule without being asked. Someone else drafts a document taking ownership of milestone deliverables. These small acts of initiative are not accidents; they're signals. The culture is shifting. What started as storming slowly morphs into norming. Ownership is moving from obligation to intention. You didn't impose it. You created space for it. And yes, taking that road makes all the difference.

Lessons from the Janitor's Closet

The best janitorial work often happens in the quiet hours, after the urgency has passed, before the credit is assigned. Like the elves in the old tale of the shoemaker, who worked unseen through the night so the cobbler could thrive, project janitors step in while others sleep, stitch things back together, and disappear before morning. The shoes are finished. The team moves forward. No one remembers the fix; they only know that things now work. That's the point. The elves didn't ask for recognition. They left no note. But the shoemaker prospered because of what was done in the dark. So it goes with fractured projects. Gratitude is never guaranteed, but the work still matters. In fact, it is often the invisible effort, the rework no one talks about, the gap quietly closed, that makes success possible. The value of the project janitor's role is rarely stated outright, but it is there, woven into every deliverable that arrives on time and every problem that never escalates.

Still, there's a reason leadership calls in a project janitor. Sometimes the elves don't show up. Significant gaps get missed, or ignored, or blamed on someone who's already gone. Days pass. Weeks. Then the letter arrives. A legal document. A Notice for Corrective Action. It doesn't shout, but it lands like the rumble of an approaching freight train. A Notice for Corrective Action. A formal warning from the client that something in the contract has failed and must be remedied. It's not a conversation. It's a chest-beating clock. A clock you cannot stop watching. You have a deadline to respond, to correct, to clean up before the partnership itself begins to fray, or worse. To a project janitor, it's less about blame and more about recognition. Someone finally noticed the mess. Now comes the question: can you clean it fast enough to keep the doors open?

The first move isn't to react. It's to breathe. A Notice for Corrective Action invites panic, but panic is sloppy. No drama. This is a moment for stoicism: not as a philosophy, but as a posture. Stay steady. Stay still. Read the letter line by line. Strip out the tone. Identify the substance. Is the issue a missed deliverable, a misinterpreted requirement, a broken process? Separate what's contractual from what's emotional. Then pull the records. Compare the claims to the facts. Most notices are written in heat, but you respond with clarity. This isn't just cleanup, it's triage.

The response must match the tone of the notice, not the tone of the meetings that came before it, or the tension it stirred. The reply is clean. Cool. It addresses only what was written. The project janitor answers the Notice for Corrective Action in sequence, with references to contract sections where applicable. No emotion. No elaboration. No "next time" or "we intend to." Respond to the points as presented, nothing more. If something is misunderstood, clarify. If something is accurate, acknowledge. Include supporting documentation when needed but never layer the response with undue interpretation. This is not about being agreeable. It's about being precise. Be precise.

The best cleanup is the one that never escalates. That's the real win. And what often goes unnoticed is that the same principles used to respond to a Notice for Corrective Action are the ones that prevent it in the first place. Calm. Precision. Documentation. A focus on what's written, not what's assumed. These aren't just reaction strategies. They're everyday disciplines. A project janitor doesn't wait for a formal dispute to show up before cleaning. The best cleanups are quiet, continuous, and methodical. Still, when those disciplines aren't shared, when the elves drift or disengage, that's when small issues begin to swell. That's when spills become rivers of rework. That's when the work becomes all too visible, far too late.

Spills and Cleanups

One of the surest ways to fail is to start cleaning without knowing why you were called in. Imagine storming into the cafeteria with a crew to patch a cracked window, while a burst pipe upstairs pours water onto the lunchroom grill. No one names the spill. No one points to the origin of the problem. Leadership just says, "Fix it." But fix what, exactly? Without context, a project janitor risks solving symptoms while the source continues unchecked. You burn time on surfaces while the foundation rots underneath. The better move is to pause, ask, and dig. What triggered your arrival? What's been said and what's been left unsaid? If no one tells you, observe until the pattern reveals itself. The mess is never just on the floor. It's in the footsteps.

The fix? Ask for the origin story. Who noticed the problem first? What patterns of failure led to your arrival? Who left and what did they leave behind? Ask these things outright or ask them quietly through observation. Look at the last ten emails. The last ignored risk. The artifact no one updated. You are not just in charge of cleaning things up. You are a pattern recognizer. Until you know where the leak began, you risk cleaning puddles that will return repeatedly. Drip. Drip. Drip.

It is not only what we do, but also what we do not do,
for which we are accountable.
-- Molière

Adding the Polish

The staffing plan reads: Engineer, Scrum Master, Project Manager. That's because no one would dare bring it to its basic truth. What leadership needs, more often than they realize, is a Project Janitor. There's no kickoff for janitorial services. You won't find 'cleanup' in the job description. But when the threads begin to fray and the tempo of the project collapses, someone gets the call. Not to redesign. Not to reimagine. To recover. The project janitor arrives without ceremony. They read the room. They notice what others step over. They find the trail of what wasn't said and follow it. Quietly. Thoroughly. Without complaint. The role doesn't come with applause. It comes with accountability.

When you step up, you aren't asked to be the face of the solution. You're asked to become the frame that holds it together. The one who steadies the team, quiets the loudness of the silence, and restores motion where momentum stalls. It's not a title. It's a stance. A discipline. A choice to lead by cleaning up what others leave behind. The project janitor isn't there to be remembered. They're there so the project itself can move forward and forget that the mess ever happened. To succeed.

Janitor's Keyring

Every project has a key no one can find. The project janitor doesn't wait for it to appear. They find a way to open the door anyway.

The Wisdom Within: The Elves and the Shoemaker

There once was a shoemaker with a failing shop. The work was honest, the skills sharp enough, but the margins were thin, and each night ran longer than the last just to keep up with demand. Orders sat unfinished. Leather scraps piled at the edges of the bench. He didn't slack; he simply ran out of time. One night, as he closed shop early with little more than hope left to inventory, he laid out the last piece of leather and sighed, "I'll try again tomorrow."

But when morning came, the shoes were already finished. They weren't just stitched, they were perfect. Quiet craftsmanship in every seam. No fanfare. No signature. Just a pair of shoes where there had been only intention. The shoemaker blinked, nodded once, and sold them. Enough to buy more leather. Enough to try again.

The next night, he did the same: set out the materials and walked away. And again, by dawn, the shoes were ready. Better than before. Orders returned. So did his reputation. The shop lived. But not because he worked harder. Because someone else had stepped in, uninvited and unnoticed, and fixed the thing before it broke for good.

He never saw them. Only shadows once. A thread left out of place. A tool moved an inch to the right. Still, he felt their presence in the rhythm returning to his work. And one day, he realized it wasn't luck but partnership, unseen.

He made them clothes. He left them a thank-you. They were always gone by morning. Job done.

That's what we do.

We don't sign our name on the shoes. We don't demand to be seen. We step in while the project sleeps. We sew what is coming apart. We leave behind momentum and store the rest in the lessons learned.

No one remembers the project janitor when the work is whole again. But they wouldn't be walking without them.

-- Brothers Grimm, as told by a Project Janitor

Adding to Your Toolbox

Absorb before you act: Start by listening, watching, and reading between the lines. Do not rush to fix. Your first job is to understand what others have learned to ignore.

Reconstruct the story: Every mess has a backstory. Find it. Trace the origin of drift through incomplete conversations, skipped steps, and habits that became norms.

Ask what brought you in: Whether anyone says it aloud or not, something triggered your arrival. Find the source. Do not clean blindly.

Watch what repeats: Missed handoffs, vague answers, slow responses. These are not isolated. They are symptoms of deeper patterns. Follow them.

Restore rhythm: Let alignment return through consistency, not command. Repeat what matters. Invite cadence through clarity.

Let purpose emerge: Do not preach vision. Point to progress. Purpose returns when people see how their work connects and begins to matter again.

Create room for trust: Offer structure, not pressure. Let the team find their footing. Celebrate forward motion, not perfection.

Write down what matters: Keep track of decisions and direction. Not for formality, but so the team does not get lost again.

Respond with calm: When tension surfaces, strip out the noise. Focus on the facts. Avoid drama. Be steady, specific, and brief.

Act when the silence shifts: You will know it is time when people stop nodding and start asking. That is your moment. Lead without ceremony.

Look for quiet ownership: Progress looks like updates made without reminders. Deliverables claimed without prompting. That is the turn.

Let others shine: If the work flows and no one notices you are there, good. That is the goal. Quiet success is the cleanest kind.

Chapter 2
Brushing Away Ambiguity: Defining the Scope of the Mess

Executive Summary

Projects don't fail because they're messy. They fail because no one defines the mess. The project janitor's first job isn't to run in and clean up, it's to learn. Name what's broken, what was promised, and what doesn't belong.

Chapter 2 reframes scope not as paperwork, but as perimeter. It walks through real-world tools and conversations that separate assumptions from agreements, wish lists from work plans. Through metaphor and experience, including a hurricane-damaged home restored only after the scope was redrawn, the chapter shows that recovery begins not with action, but with clarity.

Silence doesn't equal consent. Motion doesn't mean progress. And scope? It isn't a slipper that fits whoever wants to wear it. The project janitor doesn't force the fit. They find the shape. They draw the line. They remind the team what they were originally invited to build.

The Mess at Hand

It doesn't begin with vision. It begins with stinging in your eyes. Onions. Rotting, sharp enough to bite back, sour enough to turn your stomach. You smell something left too long unattended. A backlog bloated with half-measures. Documents marked "final" but edited six times since. No one can tell you which version to trust. Tasks stretch backward without owners. Decisions drift in group chats, undocumented and fading. Secret spreadsheets.

You weren't here for the storm, but now you're standing in its aftermath, mop in hand, asked to draw the map forward. But before you chart the route, you must name the terrain. What's broken? What's missing? What's real?

Then comes the word you'll hear too often: Critical. But when everything is critical, how can anything be? A fire in every direction leaves no path clear. Without scope, urgency becomes noise. Just noise. The mess doesn't introduce itself. It surrounds. It seeps in, disguised as normal. Your job isn't just to notice it. It's to define it. Then adjust. Because if the mess is everywhere, your effort disappears into darkness. Scope is your flashlight. Flip the switch.

The danger of poor scoping isn't always fire and collapse. Sometimes it's quiet, gradual. At first, the team tries to keep up, but tasks accumulate as the project expands long beyond the contracted intention. Expectations compound. Praise is rare, leadership direction even rarer. No one knows who's supposed to do what, or why. Deliverables blur. Priorities shift. And in the confusion, someone always ends up playing Cinderella. Left with the ash and the chores, uninvited to the ball. Not because they lacked talent, but because no one clarified the difference between cleaning the kitchen and rebuilding the kingdom. Scope creep doesn't just wreck timelines, it fractures trust, burns out the willing, and turns your best people invisible.

When you walk into a project bent and stalled of motion, don't assume the plan you're handed is accurate. Often, you inherit a patchwork of old objectives and newer pressures, partially voiced, mostly buried. Cinderella didn't need another list of chores. She didn't need a fairy godmother. She needed to ask whether the invitation had her name on it. Ask. Before the planning meetings. Before the re-baselining. Before you agree to fix what's broken, ask what was promised, what was assumed, and what's been added without consent. Naming the mess means distinguishing noise from need, critical from nice to have, intention from inheritance. You are not here to do everything. You are here to define what everything means. Scope is context, and context is the slipper that fits. Without that clarity, even the best effort is misused. Even the best team stays stuck at the hearth.

The Cleaning Strategy

Clarity begins with contrast. Before you can realign effort, you must separate the mess from the mission. That means defining two things: the scope of what's broken, and the scope of what you've really been asked to deliver. They are likely not the same. The mistake most project leaders make, especially those dropped in midstream, is trying to build the plan before understanding the perimeter. But a blueprint drawn on a dirty surface only recreates the confusion. Wipe it clean first.

Every tangled initiative has two shadows: what was originally agreed to, and what has since been assumed. Your job is to track both. Scope is not a list of tasks; it's a negotiation between capacity, expectation, and intent. It is never a paint-by-number outline of tidy requirements. It lives in ambiguity and must be interrogated. Negotiate. Project janitors don't do what we're told. We do what's right. That's not rebellion. That's responsibility. You are not here to satisfy appetite. You are here to surface alignment. And that begins with knowing the agreement and what's crept in without consent.

Begin by identifying the outer edge of the mess. What work has already been committed to, and by whom? What deliverables were promised, and to which stakeholders? What deadlines were set, and under what constraints? Until you can answer those questions clearly, the project is not under your control. You'll be reacting, not leading. A project without a defined scope doesn't pause to wait for clarity. Scope expands. The wish list grows. The effort outpaces the agreement. Then it collapses, not from failure, but from compliance. Everyone said yes. No one drew the line. Then it was midnight. No ball. Just mice.

There was a scope to the magic for Cinderella. She had a curfew, and a price for staying past it. The invitation, the contract, had terms. So it is with your project. Every deliverable, every phase, every role must be contained by a boundary the team understands. Otherwise, the story breaks. And not just for the project janitor stuck cleaning up, but for everyone burdened with work no one scoped, no one approved, and no one claimed. Have you met the developer toggling between pink and blue because no one could decide? How about the tester chasing features that were never in the contract? Yes, you have.

Scrub Away the Chaos

Scrubbing begins with definition. Not action, not velocity, but definition. And that means documentation. Documentation is the spine of the boundary, not just charters and contracts, but the real working artifacts that clarify who's doing what, why, and when. Scope isn't a sentence buried in a kickoff slide; it's the rhythm of daily decision-making. Without scope, even the most brilliant contributor ends up playing the wrong part in the wrong act of the wrong story. You can't control how the project began. But you can define what the project means from here.

And that begins with precision: the contract language, itemized requirements, gap session notes, work breakdown, detailed plans. Your job isn't to guess the line. It's to locate it, confirm it, and if needed, defend it.

Before the conversation begins, make sure the right people are in the "room." Scope clarity doesn't come from hallway whispers or side-channel chats. Bring the decision-makers, not just the doers. Include the person who signed the contract. The sponsor who set the expectations. The delivery lead who's managing the timeline. When those voices aren't present, scope becomes speculation. Once all are present, talk.

Start the conversation with calm and curiosity, not confrontation. Pull them into a shared question: "Can we walk through what was originally expected?" Let the silence do some of the work. Dead air can be revealing. Ask them to define success in their own words. Then bring out the commitments. Reference the contract, the charter, the original requirements, whatever paper trail you've found. Highlight mismatches between what was documented and what's now being asked. Not to blame, but to re-anchor. Scope recovery is not always about saying no, though you may need to. Say yes to the right things. The job is to reconnect the glittering ballroom they remember with the cinders you were handed and surface the differences with precision. Most people don't mean to overreach. They just forget where the edges are. Remind them. Gently, clearly, and in writing.

Once the conversation is underway, employ the tools that morph ambiguity back into real scope. Start with the contract. That's your anchor. Scope begins there: itemized, implied, or buried in the fine print. Don't just scan the summary. Dig into the attachments, the exhibits, the assumptions near the signature line. What was promised? To whom? Under what constraints?

Once you have that baseline, move to the work breakdown and task sequencing. Don't just skim it. Scrub it. Every work package should trace back to the contract. If it doesn't, it may be out of scope, or it may be something that was promised but never planned. Confirm that each item has an owner, a timeline, and a clear outcome. Are dependencies captured properly? Watch for vague verbs like "support" or "finalize." Such verbiage often signals placeholder thinking or scope drift. Mop it up.

Next, cross-check the contract against the documented requirements. Whether you are working in a traditional waterfall model or within an agile framework, a solid traceability of requirements helps ensure alignment from initial request to final outcome. In waterfall, the requirement traceability matrix, RTM, confirms that each contract clause maps directly to a defined deliverable. In agile, features, user stories, and other backlog items need to connect to acceptance criteria and the value delivered. If there is no traceability to requirements in place, create it. It is your thread through the maze. Even a basic spreadsheet will do. Work with your team to gather and record what was missed using notes from gap sessions, stakeholder interviews, and the undocumented decisions collected along the way. If it isn't documented, it didn't happen. If it did happen, it's your job to make sure it's documented and communicated to the appropriate staff. Cleanup is about removing clutter and rebuilding the plan and the team's confidence: one document, one line item, one truth at a time.

Lessons from the Janitor's Closet

Some cleanups start late. Others start wrong. The mess isn't just water forced in by a relentless wind. It's the contract no one reviewed, the wish list no one challenged, the scope no one defined. When scope is lost, even good intentions become liabilities. The longer ambiguity lingers, the more expensive the fix becomes. Ask Sarah. Hers is a true story.

N.G. Swampbottom Construction, a new-home builder that had pivoted into renovations after the 2004 Florida hurricanes, had already assigned a project manager, a well-meaning professional named Kyle. He launched into the residential restoration using boilerplate documents pulled from the company's new-build playbook. Kyle never truly reviewed the contract. He didn't clarify the scope. His work breakdown was filled with high-level tasks like "Mechanical Rough-In" and "Exterior Finish," but lacked proper sequencing, permit schedules, and any reference to coastal-grade materials. The project looked organized on paper, but the paper didn't match the property.

As delays mounted, Kyle became overwhelmed. When the homeowners began changing their demands, he was too eager to please. He said "yes" when the contract said "change request." He nodded when he should have clarified. But a contract has boundaries, and Kyle never found or defended the line. The result was predictable: timelines slipped, budgets blurred, and deliverables shifted without agreement. It wasn't progress. It was sequencing failure. Rooms waited on fixtures while new features jumped the line. Materials were ordered for changes no one had documented. At one point, they began painting the crown molding before installing the dining room beam, which required the entire ceiling to be torn out and replaced. Everyone thought they were helping. No one was steering.

By the time Sarah arrived, the project was already months behind schedule. Costs had ballooned. Trust had eroded. She didn't begin with apologies. She began with scope. Clipboard in hand, she walked the perimeter of the mess, inside and out. She documented what had been damaged, what had been started, what had gone wrong, and what had been promised. Then she sat with the homeowners and pulled out the original contract, comparing it line by line against the work breakdown Kyle had assembled. The gaps appeared immediately: sequencing errors, missing permit timelines, and no reference to local building code or material grade. Critical components had never made it from contract to plan.

She didn't panic. She adjusted. Using the original contract as her baseline, Sarah rebuilt the work breakdown structure (WBS) from scratch, this time anchored in real scope and real-world constraints. She documented every detail including phases, inspections, permits, and material lead times. Then she met with the homeowners and walked them through each task. Line by line, she showed where expectations had outpaced agreement. She found the line. If it was promised but never planned, she pulled it back in. If it was requested but never contracted, she set it aside for change control. Scope creep wasn't stopped by saying no. It was stopped by making the boundary visible again. She defended the line. Once the edges were clear, progress resumed. Trade teams stopped tripping over each other. Work aligned. Momentum returned. The project didn't just recover, it stabilized. No wand. No spell. Just clarity.

Spills and Cleanups

Don't Let Silence Turn into the Contract

Scope rarely explodes. It seeps. A favor here, a task there. A small "yes" offered in the spirit of helpfulness. A nod given without clarification. You don't mean to take it all on, but you do. And the silence? It gets read as agreement.

That's how Cinderella ended up in the ashes. Not with a whip, but with a list. The stepmother didn't redraw the rules. She simply added to them, slowly, until the original role vanished beneath the weight of unspoken expectations. And Cinderella, so capable, so compliant, never challenged the scope. She accepted every new task, every shifting direction, until she no longer existed to her stepsisters except as labor.

Sound familiar? A leader of a failing project sees the creep but says nothing. Sees the work expand but lets it roll forward to preserve harmony. It feels easier to adjust quietly than to confront publicly. Until the moment comes when you're expected to deliver something no one ever formally asked for, and your silence is held up as consent.

Your silence will not protect you.
-- Audre Lorde

Don't let silence write your contract. Speak up. Clarify. Re-anchor. That isn't defiance. That's stewardship.

Adding the Polish

Projects don't fall apart because they're messy. They fall apart when no one defines the mess. The project janitor begins by noticing what others step over: what's broken, what was promised, and what doesn't belong. Scope isn't the paperwork. It's the quiet, polished shape of the work. If that shape fades, tasks multiply. Priorities shift. People stretch to cover the gaps. Someone always ends up in the ashes because the boundary was never held.

Cleanup starts by restoring that boundary. You gather the right people. You revisit the contract. You ask the questions no one has asked in a while. That's what Sarah did. She clarified what the work was supposed to be. And once that was clear, the team could move again without ambiguity. The project janitor need not raise their voice. They need to mark the edges. Find and keep the shape. Because once agreed, scope doesn't stretch. It fits, or it doesn't.

Janitor's Keyring

Scope isn't a fitted slipper. It doesn't stretch to fit ambition. It fits or it doesn't. The janitor doesn't force the shoe. They find the foot it was made for and leave the rest behind.

The Wisdom Within: A Cinderella Story

Once there was a house with no project leader or plan. No defined roles. No boundaries. Just a widowed father, a second wife, and three girls, two who gave orders, and one who carried the weight.

Cinderella wasn't hired. She wasn't asked. She was absorbed. Tasks accumulated like dust. First the floors, then the meals, then the mending. No scope was defined, so everything became hers. No timeline was drawn, so the work never stopped. And no one pushed back, least of all her.

The stepsisters weren't villains. They were opportunists in a system with no guardrails. They saw someone saying yes and kept handing her more. The stepmother didn't scream. She delegated. Quietly. Relentlessly. Every new task arrived like a favor. Every favor became expectation. No change requests. Just scope, expanding silently in every direction.

Then came the announcement. A royal ball. One evening. One deliverable: show up dressed and ready.

The stepsisters had approval. They had resources. They had visible roles to play. Cinderella had none of these. Still, she wanted to go. Not to take over. Just to be seen.

Cinderella asked. Her request was denied. Not rejected formally, just buried under a heap of new tasks. Sweep the hearth. Hem the gowns. Re-iron the napkins. She was busy with work that no one tracked, delivering outcomes no one valued.

And yet, she found help. Not from leadership, but from an outside stakeholder with an unconventional toolkit. A fairy godmother with no budget constraints yet limited runway. The timeline was fixed. Midnight. No extensions, no buffer, and no excuses were allowed. Deliverables would vanish if mismanaged.

Cinderella made it. She delivered. Stunning. For a moment, everything aligned.

But the clock struck twelve, and all deliverables came due. Time expired.

What remained wasn't the gown or the title, but a single glass slipper. A record of what was once promised, and a test to see who could match it. And the prince began to garner input from his stakeholders.

Many tried to force the fit. But scope never stretches. It either matches the work or it doesn't.

And when they reached Cinderella, tired, quiet, overlooked, she didn't make a speech. She just tried on the shoe.

It fit.

Not because she wanted it most. So much more. She didn't just fit the scope. She embodied it. The work, the patience, the alignment was always hers. She *was* the scope all along.

-- Brothers Grimm, as told by a Project Janitor

Adding to Your Toolbox

Identify the mess: Do not clean blindly. Define what is broken, missing, or misunderstood before acting. Clarity must come first.

Challenge the word *critical*: When everything is urgent, nothing is. Ask whether the task supports the goal or simply fills the silence.

PLAYBOOK FOR PROJECT JANITORS

Ask what was promised: Before fixing, ask what was originally agreed upon. Surface the difference between expectation and commitment.

Stop the seep: Scope does not explode. It creeps. Say yes to what fits. Say no, or not yet, to what doesn't. Silence is not consent.

Draw the line: Scope is not the same as effort. Separate what was agreed to from what was assumed. If the work has no boundary, it has no meaning.

Locate the edges: Identify deliverables, ownership, deadlines, and constraints. If you can't name them cleanly, you can't protect them.

Gather the right people: Clarity requires decision-makers. Do not define scope in isolation. Confirm understanding across roles.

Use calm to confront: Start the conversation with curiosity, not blame. Ask what success was supposed to look like. Then check the trail.

Verify with documentation: Scope is not a feeling. It is found in the paper trail. Contracts. Requirements. Notes. Dig for it.

Check the plan against the promise: Every item of work should be tied back to what was agreed. If it doesn't, ask why. If no one knows, remove it or reframe it.

Spot vague language: Watch for words like *support* or *finalize* that sound productive but hide uncertainty. Ask who is doing what, by when, and to what standard. Vague language invites divergence from the goal. Specifics restore control.

Clarify to restore momentum: Do not build on top of assumptions. Before things speed up, make sure they are aimed in the right direction.

Defend the boundary: You are not here to do everything. You are here to define what everything means and hold the line. That's what keeps the story from falling apart.

Chapter 3
Sweeping With Purpose: Building a Clear Vision

Executive Summary

Projects don't fail because the team isn't working. They fail because no one agrees on where they're headed. The project janitor's job isn't just to observe, it's to uncover the vision and make it visible. This chapter reframes vision not as an abstract ideal, but as a process that emerges through observation, dialogue, and alignment. The project janitor traces the patterns that wear the team down, identifying where the vision has been lost or bent. Through real-world examples, including the restoration of the Leaning Tower of Pisa, the chapter shows how vision isn't a one-time declaration, it's something to be revisited, adjusted, and maintained. Just as a project team needs a clear direction, it also needs consistent focus to stay aligned. Without vision, effort becomes directionless. But when the vision is clear, every task can be tested against it, every decision aligned with it. The chapter ends with a simple but impactful reminder: vision is not what you hope to build, but what you're still willing to uphold when everything begins to lean.

The Mess at Hand

It begins with motion. Not the kind that stirs progress, but the kind that kicks up dust. You know that dust, movement for movement's sake, unanchored and undirected. Floating. Meetings fill calendars, tasks shift between hands, documents change version numbers, yet the outcome remains indistinct. There is effort, even urgency, but no shared image of what completion looks like. You may have even polished the scope, found the edges, defended the line. Still, there's dust. The floor is swept, but no one can say whether it's clean. Why? Because without vision, motion becomes mimicry, work rehearsed without resolution, activity that exhausts but does not align. The team moves, yes, but sideways. Updates replace insight. And beneath the noise masquerading as progress, the original mess waits, untouched and unnamed.

Sometimes the team feels it. Sometimes they don't. The symptoms vary. Questions go unanswered not because no one knows, but because no one agrees. Decisions contradict each other. Priorities shift without a center. Work gets redone not from incompetence; yes, sometimes from incompetence, but more often from the absence of shared direction. It's easy to confuse this situation with chaos, but chaos at least admits it has no pattern. This is something more subtle. A kind of elegant disarray, where everyone is diligently pushing a broom even though they don't know where the dirt is. Vision is what connects those parts. Without it, even the most efficient efforts unravel. Not from lack of skill; yes, sometimes from that too, but more often from lack of shared understanding.

The symptoms persist because no one names the pattern. Everyone sees their piece, but no one steps back to frame the whole. When vision is missing, process breaks down in ways that aren't always obvious at first. Tasks get done, but not in the right order. Approvals pile up while dependencies go untracked. Workflows exist, but no one trusts them. Teams adapt around inefficiency until dysfunction feels routine. Over time, those shortcuts become the system. Teams adapt around inefficiency until dysfunction feels routine. Meetings repeat. Reports echo. But nothing ties back to a common outcome. Without vision, the process loses shape. And once that shape is lost, no amount of effort restores it without stepping back to see what was meant to be built in the first place.

Patterns form whether we see them or not. Sometimes, the project looks fine on the surface. The tickets move, the statuses progress, the meetings end on time. But atop that polished floor, walker's shoes are wearing out. Something is being expended in silence. Energy drains, timelines stretch, trust thins. And yet no one can put a finger on quite why. That's when the project janitor needs to look closer. Not at what is visible, but at what repeats. The unexplained fatigue. The tasks that never stay closed. The quiet questions left unanswered. When the mess refuses to name itself, your job is not to fix harder. Your job is to observe. Observe.

Observation is not passive; it's active patience. It means tracking the worn paths others overlook. Noticing which conversations loop without landing, which deliverables never feel done, which team members always look tired but never ask for help. You are not just watching; you are tracking. Beneath every repeated misstep lies a choice made long ago, perhaps for a good reason, perhaps for no reason at all. The point is not to assign blame. The point is to follow the wear. Shoes don't shred themselves. Something is leading them across that same floor, night after night, task after task, until the soles vanish and no one remembers what the steps were for.

Still, at some point, watching isn't even enough. You need to record what you see. Not just the symptoms, but the underlying process, the routines, handoffs and assumptions that allow them to persist. Vision doesn't arrive as inspiration. Instead, it emerges from the patterns you've traced, the questions you've asked, the truths no one else has had the time or courage to say aloud. A strong vision doesn't float above the mess. It takes shape inside it. You begin to draw it not with lofty words but grounded in sound intentions and actions. Is this process working? Where are we headed? What is the definition of "done"? Until those answers are shared, the work stays stuck in repetition, burning through shoes one quiet night at a time.

Just like the Twelve Dancing Princesses, the real answer isn't in the room. It's in the path they keep returning to when no one is looking. The worn shoes tell a story, but what if no one's listening? The team delivers, revises, delivers again. Their effort is visible. The drain is not. That's when the project janitor stops watching and starts tracking. You follow the steps no one talks about. You track the trail after hours, through handoffs and half-told decisions. What you find is rarely sabotage. It's habit. Hidden loops, buried logic, routines that feel like progress but never arrive. The mystery isn't in the outcome. It's in the repetition. Follow the worn path. Arrive at a vision.

The Cleaning Strategy

Vision is not always a declaration, but it is always a process. Wander or walk with purpose. The work of building it begins not in the boardroom but in the hallway, in the sprint review, in the silences between standup and delivery. A project janitor doesn't impose direction. They uncover it. Piece by piece, they assemble what no one else has had the time to gather. The gaps in conversation. The contradictions in planning. The hesitations when someone says, "That's how we did it last time." Building a clear vision means starting with what's true, even when the conversation is uncomfortable. Especially when it is.

To build vision is to test understanding out loud. Not to proclaim, but to propose. Read a line from the meeting notes, the actions or decisions, perhaps. Then ask, "Is this what we mean?" Invite correction. Expect disagreement. Vision cannot be assigned; it must be confirmed. You're not aiming for consensus on every detail. You're aiming for shared direction, a picture that orients the team even when the specifics are still forming. But building vision is only the beginning. It must be championed. It must be maintained. Without stewardship, vision recedes into slides and slogans. Alignment doesn't begin with certainty. It begins with language. Speak the draft. Let others sharpen it. If they can see it, they can shape it. If they shape it, they can follow it. Make it their idea.

In the story of the Twelve Dancing Princesses, no one could explain why their shoes wore out each night. The king offered a reward to anyone who could solve the mystery. Many tried. All failed, except one. One soldier stopped guessing and started watching. He followed their path in silence, tracing the hidden steps they took underground, night after night, to a place no one had dared to look. Projects are no different. Effort is spent. Time disappears. The team is tired, and no one can say quite why. But if you can follow the loop, if you can trace the invisible staircase beneath the workflow, you can reveal the truth behind the wear. That's where adjusting the vision begins, not in what people say they're doing, but in what they repeat when no one's watching.

Adjusting the vision doesn't mean rewriting the charter. It means aligning the mop with the bucket. You start with what the team is actually doing, then ask whether those actions, or inactions, match what was intended. If the gap is wide, don't panic. Don't point fingers. Mark it. Share it. Help the team see the contrast. Most misalignment isn't malicious. It's accumulated. A deadline here, a workaround there, a deliverable padded with shortcut language to buy time. Slowly, the work wends off course until the project feels misaligned, and no one can quite say when it happened. Vision work means asking the sweeping question again and again: "Is this still the right path?" And if not, "What's the next thing we need to do to shine this floor into one worth walking across?"

A clear vision doesn't live in a slide deck. It lives in the calendar, the backlog, the checklist before deployment. Vision carries across phases and meetings, documents and tools, without changing shape. Consistency is the true test. The story told in the kickoff should still be evident in the daily standup, in the sprint review, in the project closeout report. When the vision holds across artifacts, the team begins to trust it. It becomes the familiar filter by which we make decisions and measure our steps. "Does this task move us toward the picture we agreed on?" "Is this still the right use of our effort?" When vision takes root, the project begins to align on its own. Not because someone is enforcing it, but because the path has been made clear enough to follow.

Scrub Away the Chaos

Sustaining vision means more than repeating it. It means maintaining the environment where it can thrive. That includes guarding against noise, such as new requests, shifting priorities, vague praise, or leadership drift. Every project is a workplace cluttered with distraction. Scrub away the chaos. Vision needs weight to hold steady. Anchor it in documentation but reinforce it in conversation. Ask the same questions until the answers stay the same. Revisit the goals not just at phase gates, but when something starts to feel like it's time to buff the tarnish. Consistency doesn't mean rigidity. It means being faithful to the picture you agreed on, even as the work evolves. That's how vision holds, not through force, but through a thoughtful pattern.

Begin where the friction shows. Not in the vision document, but in the hallway conversation that doesn't match it. In the task that no one owns. In the status update that sounds like progress but avoids commitment. Scrubbing a broken process starts with identifying where alignment is breaking down. Look for the steps where rework lives. Ask what keeps getting postponed, reassigned, or debated. These aren't just inefficiencies, they're indicators. They show you where the vision is failing to take hold or never landed in the first place. Don't start with what's out of place. Start with what keeps going in circles. Scrub.

Scrubbing doesn't mean halting the work. It means slowing just enough to inspect the motion. Take one process, one artifact, one ritual, and hold it up to the vision. Ask: "Is this helping us move forward, or are we just polishing what no longer belongs?" Still, not everything broken needs to be replaced. Some tools just need to be rinsed, refactored, or realigned. Cleaning isn't always dramatic. Sometimes it means reducing steps. Sometimes it means naming the one that's being done right but was never written down. Don't aim for reinvention. Forget perfection. Aim for clarity. That's what keeps the floor clean.

To clarify vision from chaos, start by anchoring it to something real. Pull a current deliverable. Open the task tracker. Find a recent decision made under pressure. Ask the team to describe what success looks like for that item, in their own words. Then ask them to connect it back to the big picture. If the answers vary, the vision isn't clear yet. Don't correct them. Don't present the answer. Just hold the mirror steady. The goal isn't to dictate alignment. It's to surface the gaps. That's how shared understanding begins: not in declaration, but in reflection.

Once the gaps are visible, document what was said. Not as a transcript, but as a shared draft. Create a one-paragraph summary of the vision as the team sees it. Share it back. Ask again: "Does this still sound right?" Make revisions in the open. When the team begins to nod without hesitation, write it down. Then make it visible. Put it in the backlog. Reference it in the status report. Pull a quote from it into the next deck. Encapsulating a large, complex project in a few lines isn't easy, but businesses do this all the time. A mission, a mantra, a headline on a wall. They use vision to drive alignment across departments, years, even generations. A project is no different. Without a unifying statement, tasks become isolated and decisions drift. But when the vision is known, every step, handoff, and change request can be tested against it. That's not decoration. That's direction.

For example: "This project will simplify how frontline staff engage with clients, fewer systems, fewer steps, more time for the work that matters." That line may seem small, but it's not the product. It's the proof. This chapter is the work it takes to get there. When that vision begins to echo in meetings, in emails, and on whiteboards, the team stops coding in isolation and starts delivering with purpose. Vision becomes real. Not because you declared it, but because they recognized it. They shared it.

Lessons from the Janitor's Closet

Not all messes are recent. Some are inherited. Some are centuries old.

When construction began on the Leaning Tower of Pisa in 1173, the intent was clear. Ancient engineers wanted to build a bell tower to demonstrate architectural splendor. But vision without grounding can falter fast, literally. Early builders laid the foundation in soft, unstable soil. By the time the second floor was underway, the structure had already begun to tilt. They tried to compensate by making one side of the upper levels taller than the other. The result: a spiraling misalignment that became both infamous and irreversible.

Work stopped. Work restarted. Then stopped again. Wars intervened. Budgets collapsed. Engineers came and went, each with their own theory, none with a solution. What was once a symbol of civic pride became a monument to cluttered thinking. The vision had tarnished. And with no one to own that vision, the project tilted further out of alignment.

Centuries later, in the 1990s, a new team approached the problem not with spectacle, but with clarity and restraint. They didn't try to straighten the tower. They didn't rewrite history. They sought to preserve it. The implied vision was simple: stabilize the structure without erasing what it had become. Through years of study and care, they reduced the lean by over 17 inches. Engineers extracted soil, counterweighted the base, and strengthened the foundation without altering the tower's character. Their work extended the life of the landmark by at least 300 years. Today, the tower remains open to visitors. It stands not just as a monument to medieval ambition, but as proof that a leaning project can still serve its purpose if someone takes the time to steady it.

A project janitor doesn't rebuild for glory. They steady what still stands. They don't chase a new vision to cover the dirty, aging one. They realign what still matters: the process, the vision, the original purpose. They inherit the tilt, trace the pattern, and clear the dust that's hidden in plain sight, even when the shoes are already worn.

Vision is not just what you hope to build. It's what you're still willing to uphold once everything begins to lean.

Spills and Cleanups

The most common mistake isn't vision drift. It's pretending vision was never needed in the first place. A team gets behind schedule, pressure builds, and suddenly clarity feels like a luxury. The slide deck gets shortened. The conversation gets cut. The sprint gets planned, but stories fall off due to a conspiracy of messy incidents. Few project management courses, frameworks, or handbooks even pause long enough to ask what the vision really is. They teach how to schedule the work, not how to envision it. Yet without vision, the team doesn't slow down. They just move in the wrong direction. Tasks get checked off. Reports look full of color. But effort begins to pool in the corners. That's when expectations are missed, or worse, land without impact.

It's the same mistake the king made in the tale of the Twelve Dancing Princesses. The shoes kept wearing out. The problem kept repeating. Night after night, the signs were there. But no one followed the steps. No one traced the path. They brought in experts, issued warnings, and chased explanations. Still, no one stopped long enough to truly observe. Until one soldier did. He watched in silence. He paid attention to what repeated, not just what was said. And slowly, the hidden pattern revealed itself. That's how the mystery was solved. Not in a rush, not in noise, but with clarity, patience, and a willingness to believe that worn shoes mean something.

So, when patterns persist, pay attention. Listen to the shoes.

Chi va piano, va sano e va lontano.
He who goes slowly, goes safely and goes far.
-- Traditional Italian proverb

Adding the Polish

Vision isn't something you declare once. It's something you return to, again and again, until the team can walk in it without asking where they're going. It doesn't need to be loud. It needs to be shared. You don't uncover it by rushing. You uncover it by noticing what repeats, what wears out, what still matters. Sometimes that's a sprint story. Sometimes it's a step in the process no one questions. Sometimes it's a worn pair of shoes at the edge of the workflow. When vision is clear, every step adds up. Not because someone enforced it, but because the path made sense.

That's what it means to sweep with purpose. You're not just moving things out of the way. You're clearing the ground so the team can move forward, together, toward something they've chosen to believe in. The vision.

Janitor's Keyring

You don't need to invent the vision. You need to reveal it, return to it, and keep it visible long enough for others to walk in it. Clarity is more than a chart or a graph. It's the vision swept with purpose.

The Wisdom Within: The Twelve Dancing Princesses

Once, in a quiet corner of the kingdom, there was a king who had twelve daughters. They were beautiful, lively, and full of energy, but their shoes were always worn out, day after day, night after night. The king could never understand it. The shoes would be torn to tatters each morning, as if they had danced through the night, but when he asked them where they'd gone, they would say nothing.

He offered a reward, a great reward, to anyone who could solve the mystery of the worn shoes. One by one, many came to try. Scholars, sages, and so-called experts arrived. They examined the shoes, questioned the princesses, and followed their every step. They all failed. The mystery deepened. The shoes kept wearing out, and still, no one could explain why.

In his frustration, the king turned to the people, seeking answers from those who had the most time to observe, those who had been quietly cleaning up the mess for years. A humble soldier, unnoticed by many, stepped forward. He didn't try to guess. He didn't try to solve the puzzle with half-measures or assumptions. He simply stopped. He stood still and watched. Not with expectation, but with patience.

Night after night, he followed the princesses as they disappeared into their chambers. He noticed something: the pattern wasn't random. There was a rhythm. The shoes didn't wear out by chance. Every night, the princesses followed a path, a familiar one. They slipped into hidden doors, walked down secret stairs, and disappeared into a world no one had seen before. It was not magic. It was a method. A process. They danced, not out of whimsy, but out of habit, a habit no one had stopped to see.

The soldier followed the pattern. He traced the hidden steps. He noticed the repetitive nature of the mess, the steps taken over and over again. They weren't trying to hide. They just didn't know anyone was paying attention.

And once the soldier had seen it, once the pattern was clear, he exposed it. He didn't reveal it with force. He simply spoke it aloud. He showed the king the path, and with that clarity, the mystery unraveled. The princesses no longer needed to hide their steps. They had been dancing in circles, but not for lack of awareness, just for lack of someone to identify it.

Just like the soldier, the project janitor's task isn't to solve the mystery of the worn shoes. It's to see the pattern, to trace the steps that others miss, and to name the process that no one has dared to question. A project janitor doesn't just clean. They observe. They listen. They see the loops, the inefficiencies, the habits that hold teams in place without them ever knowing why.

Vision doesn't live in the grand gestures or the loud declarations. It lives in the steps, the consistent, steady steps that, when followed, lead somewhere real. A project isn't about chasing new frivolous dances. It's about steadying the steps of the dance that matters.

And when the project janitor stops to listen to the shoes, to the silence, to the repeated rhythm, that's when the vision becomes clear. Not through noise, but through patience. And that's how the real work begins.

-- Brothers Grimm, as told by a Project Janitor

Adding to Your Toolbox

Observe what repeats: Not all messes announce themselves. Patterns often appear in silence, fatigue, and rework. Watch closely before you act.

Trace the wear: Notice which steps get retraced, which tasks never stay closed, which team members are burning out. Repetition reveals misalignment.

Follow the loop: Don't settle for noise or surface effort. Track the routines that waste time and wear down progress. That's where vision is hiding.

Propose, don't proclaim: Test direction out loud. Share your draft understanding and invite corrections. Vision is confirmed through feedback, not force.

Draw it from the work: Vision isn't abstract. It emerges from the real steps being taken. Ground it in observed truth, not imagined perfection.

Mark the misalignments: When effort and outcome don't match, show the gap. Don't blame. Don't spin. Just hold the mirror.

Write what's said: Document the shared language the team begins to use. Capture the draft. Let them refine it. When the agreements are real, publish it.

Anchor in simplicity: Distill the vision into a few true lines. Enough to remember. Enough to steer by. If they can recall it, they can live it.

Make it visible: Once you have alignment, reflect it in meetings, emails, trackers, and tools. Vision should echo quietly across the work.

Scrub where vision fades: Begin where friction lives. The status update with no clarity. The repeated delay. The untethered request. That's your starting point.

Refactor the broken steps: Not everything misaligned needs to be replaced. Some tools just need rinsing and realignment. Clean with care, not anger.

Return to it often: Vision isn't one and done. It must be re-seen and re-shared until it becomes the patten for every step taken.

Chapter 4
Spinning Expectations: Shaping Stakeholder Priorities with Precision

Executive Summary

High expectations aren't the problem. Misaligned ones are. Chapter 4 examines what happens when stakeholder priorities go unchecked, and the expectations of the original plan linger long after the project has changed. When sponsors ask for moon landings while the capsule loses power, someone needs to reset the goal without shaking the team. That is where the spin cycle begins. Not as manipulation, but as measured reframing. Influence with intention.

This chapter gives the project janitor tools to address stakeholder dissatisfaction with clarity and calm. It walks through real-world strategies for inspecting contracts, resetting interpretations, and influencing outcomes without taking the credit. Drawing from the story of Apollo 13 and the fable of Hansel and Gretel, it shows that recovery does not come from magic or heroics. It comes from timing, restraint, and helping others see what is no longer working, and what will.

When done right, the path forward is not forced. It is revealed. And the project does not just survive. It lands with precision.

The Mess at Hand

Pride came first. The trajectory was familiar, the objectives rehearsed. Apollo 13 stood as the next in a line of lunar victories, less a question of possibility than of polish. Apollo 11 had planted the flag. Apollo 12 had proven it wasn't a fluke. Apollo 13 was to be confirmation, refinement, routine. The language from leadership echoed assurance. The press readied headlines before the rocket cleared the tower. Success spilled into assumption, and the mission was expected to shine like a moonbeam on the ocean, gleaming with the confidence of those who believed the work was already done.

The explosion shattered more than hardware. When the oxygen tank failed, the mission lost more than a lunar objective. It lost its shape. Priorities collapsed inward. The goal could no longer be about touching the Moon. It had to become about touching Earth again. Every checklist, every timeline, every neatly plotted milestone became irrelevant. Resources diminished by the hour. Systems cascaded toward failure. The plan could no longer be followed. It had to be abandoned and rebuilt mid-flight, without margin, without precedent. What remained was priority.

Stakeholders outside the capsule were slower to realign. Their questions still pointed toward the mission they believed was underway. They asked about landing sequences while the cabin was without power. They referenced deliverables while the crew fought for air. For air. Stakeholder expectations had drifted far from the operational truth. No one had the time to revisit scope or margin to write a new vision statement. The team had to act immediately, reshaping priorities.

This is the nature of misaligned expectation. It lingers in the space between what's needed and what's demanded. It praises progress that no longer applies. It asks for metrics on work that no longer matters. The danger lies in continuing to steer toward goals that have already been swept away, mistaking momentum for direction. When a team is told to keep scrubbing while the floor gives way beneath them, no amount of soap can stop the collapse.

Not every project is an Apollo 13. But some are. Still, every project eventually faces a turning point, a tight, truth-revealing bottleneck. Sometimes it arrives in chaos. Sometimes it arrives in silence. Either way, it has the power to rewrite the purpose of the work. The old rules no longer apply, but the demands still echo. Leaders continue to ask if the website is launching, if the presentation is on track, if the milestone still holds, as if it hasn't been swept out of place with every shuffle of the broom. Behind the scenes, the team already knows the truth. The mission has changed.

The Cleaning Strategy

There's a moment in every messy project when the air feels clean again, perhaps just for a beat, until a dissatisfied stakeholder walks in and kicks up what was never fully swept away. No matter how well you frame the plan, chart the timeline, or define the scope, someone will still feel shortchanged. Maybe they weren't consulted early enough. Maybe their expectations drifted. Or maybe they simply didn't read the label on the detergent. Either way, the project janitor doesn't flinch. This is the spin cycle. It isn't punishment. It's process. When expectations collide with reality, it's not enough to defend the floorplan. You re-walk the site. You revisit the agreement. You reframe what was agreed upon in the light of what's been done. Not to deflect, but to clarify. Not to appease, but to align. This isn't about politics. It's about precision, turning a swirl of dissatisfaction into a shared understanding, one careful rotation at a time.

The first move is not to explain, but to examine. Misalignment rarely begins out of spite. It begins with ambiguity. Somewhere in the contract, in the email thread, in the versioning of a scope document, something was left unclear, or worse, assumed. The project janitor's task is not to win the argument, but to understand where the spills began. That means pulling the original agreement off the shelf, dusting off the scope, and scanning the corners for anything that might have shifted. A phrase open to interpretation. A deliverable with no clear owner. A milestone that was circled then forgotten in a ticket accidentally closed. Before anything can be clarified for others, it must be understood by you. Precision doesn't begin with correction. It begins with inspection.

Once the root of the rubble is clear, the work shifts from inspection to interpretation. Not softening. Honest reframing. Sometimes the contract says one thing but was written with another interpretation in mind. Sometimes the scope tells a story the team no longer remembers writing, let alone discussing one afternoon two years ago. The project janitor doesn't erase the past. They contextualize it. They remind the stakeholder what was said, what was meant, and where the two diverged. A disagreement about progress often hides a deeper disagreement about definition. Clarify that, and the heat begins to fade. The conversation moves from tension to terms. Negotiate.

Sometimes, the best way to handle dissatisfaction is to prevent it from surfacing in the first place. Don't dodge hard conversations. Instead, have them early, before the meeting, before the pushback, before expectations harden. The project janitor doesn't wait for objections to be raised in public. They move quietly, one conversation at a time, checking in, listening for friction, clearing confusion while it's still soft underfoot. In Japan, this practice is called nemawashi, preparing the roots before moving the tree. It means consulting stakeholders individually, gathering their input, and laying the groundwork for shared understanding long before a formal decision is made. Done well, this behind-the-scenes alignment keeps the project steady when it matters most.

Think of Hansel and Gretel. The danger wasn't just the forest, it was walking into it without agreement, without shared direction. They dropped crumbs to mark the way back, but no one confirmed the path before they left. No one aligned on the plan. That's what nemawashi prevents. It's not about leaving markers behind in case things go wrong. It's about having the right conversations before you enter the woods. The project janitor doesn't wait until the team is lost to start asking questions. They speak with each stakeholder quietly, one by one, checking expectations, surfacing concerns, and shaping the path together, before anyone steps into the unknown.

But even with planning, the trail doesn't always hold. Hansel and Gretel did their part. They tried to leave a path. Still, the breadcrumbs vanished. The environment changed. The plan was no longer useful. That's the second lesson. The project janitor knows that expectations, once set, still need to be revisited. No single meeting, no signed document, no moment of consensus is permanent. Winds shift. Stakeholders change roles. Priorities rot like candy left too long in the sun. What began as clarity becomes illusion if it isn't maintained. The project janitor checks the trail again, not to retrace steps, but to make sure the team hasn't wandered into someone else's story.

The escape didn't come from magic. It came from clarity and timing. Gretel didn't argue with the witch. She waited. She listened. Then she acted. That's the project janitor's next move: recognizing when the story has shifted and guiding the outcome without grabbing the spotlight. When expectations drift toward illusion, the project janitor doesn't call it out with fanfare. They open a path, ask the right questions, and let the stakeholder turn the key. The goal isn't to reject the candy house. It's to help the sponsor see it as a distraction, and believe the redirection was theirs all along. Influence, not authority. Presence, not credit. That's how the project turns, and how trust survives the turn.

Scrub Away the Chaos

Spinning expectations are polished through preparation, presence, and quiet follow-through. The dissatisfied stakeholder isn't the problem. Team misalignment is. And misalignment doesn't just go away after one shined conversation. It reappears, subtly and repeatedly, in assumptions, language, dashboards, and decks. That's why the project janitor doesn't leave the room once expectations are reset. They stay close. They keep the cloth damp and ready to spit-shine again. They watch how the narrative reforms, because even when agreement is reached, the residue of the old story sticks to the edges. Unforgotten.

This is where the real cleanup begins. Confrontation gives way to confirmation. Restate what was agreed to. Summarize it in plain language. Write it down. Send the follow-up. Do more than document. Anchor. Not every stakeholder remembers the same meeting the same way. Some remember what they wanted to hear. Stakeholders often do. The project janitor's job is to table the debate, scrub, rinse, and repeat. Clarity doesn't live in the room. It lives in the repetition of the recap.

Even after the escape, the forest didn't vanish. Hansel and Gretel still had to walk back through it, step by uncertain step. That's the part no one quotes. The oven gets the drama, but the real work was the journey home. The project janitor understands this. Even after consensus is reached, the project still lives in shifting terrain. Memory fades. Promises drift. Expectations creep back in like fog through the trees. That's why the project janitor doesn't just solve the immediate problem. They check the path home. They follow up. They sweep away the trail behind them, so the next step forward doesn't land in the same mud. Cleanup isn't a moment. It's a pattern. And the job isn't done until the path is clear, and the mission makes it back intact.

Lessons from the Janitor's Closet

The plan was to land on the Moon. Apollo 13 was to be the third success in a growing line of lunar achievements. The hardware had improved. The procedures had matured. The staff training could not have been better. Mission control knew the playbook, forward and back. The press was already writing headlines. But then came the rupture. An oxygen tank exploded, crippling the spacecraft. Power drained. Heat vanished. Systems failed one by one. In seconds, the mission collapsed, not just physically, but conceptually. The goal was no longer to land. The goal was to survive.

The world remembers the astronauts' calm, the famous words: "Houston, we've had a problem," and the return that should not have been possible. But behind the scenes, there was another cleanup in progress. While the astronauts held steady in silence and cold, it was the team on the ground that took to the mop. The right minds engaged immediately without hesitation, gathering specs, test rigs, checklists, and environmental readouts, sweeping everything into action. Plans were stripped down. Power cycles recalculated. Procedures re-sequenced. Stakeholders didn't call the shots now. Physics did.

Above the Earth, the spill took a different shape. The astronauts became project janitors themselves, assembling makeshift solutions from whatever the capsule carried. Plastic bags. Flight manuals. Cardboard. A sock. A roll of duct tape. Ground control walked them through the steps to build an adapter that could clean the air before it turned lethal. It wasn't elegant, but it worked. They rerouted hoses. Conserved power. Shut down systems and learned to operate in the dark. The flight plan no longer mattered. The old mission was gone. What remained was discipline, trust, and the quiet willingness to fix what could be fixed, one taped-up solution at a time.

Gene Kranz didn't give speeches, redesign the mission, or cling to the stakeholders' original plan. He redefined success. He gathered his team, reviewed the constraints, and turned questions into actions. What do we have? What can we shut down? What can we bypass? What will get us home? While the world waited for updates, he and his engineers quietly scrubbed every unnecessary expectation from the plan until only one remained: bring them back alive.

That's what a project janitor does. They keep the team calm in the capsule. They don't chase blame. They spin expectations and reframe priorities. They adapt the plan mid-flight, knowing that alignment under pressure matters more than ceremony. And when it works, it doesn't look like heroism. It looks like recovery. Quiet. Technical. Focused. Success isn't always the Moon landing. Sometimes it's the landing, period.

Spills and Cleanups

The greatest risk in a high-stakes project isn't failure. It's allowing stakeholders to cling to a version of the plan that no longer matches the work. Scope can change. Priorities can shift. But when expectations stay frozen in an earlier frame, teams keep scrubbing the tile they're told to, even when the damage has moved somewhere else. Sponsors still ask for the original milestones. Leaders still quote old estimates. Project managers get tempted to smile, nod, and try to keep the old expectations alive, even after the floor has collapsed beneath them.

That's the spill: pretending the mission is still about landing on the Moon, even as the power drains and the air runs thin.

The cleanup begins with redefinition. That's what Gene Kranz provided. He set the expectation. He didn't insist the original plan could hold. He didn't wait for permission to shift the goal. He scrubbed away every part of the plan that no longer served the team or the moment. What remained was a single, shared, achievable objective: bring them home alive.

And that's why his famous quote, "Failure is not an option," still resonates. Even though it wasn't spoken in the heat of the mission, it captures the mindset of the project janitor under pressure. You can't afford to panic. You can't afford to stall. You clean what you can. Strip away what doesn't help. And keep the team moving. Quietly. Intentionally. You bring them home.

We just kept going. We knew what we had to do, and we did it.
We never gave up on the crew or the mission.
-- Gene Kranz, Flight Director, Apollo 13

Adding the Polish

Projects don't collapse under ambition. They bend under the weight of expectations left unchecked. The project janitor doesn't resist vision. They clear space for it to take shape. They sweep the clutter from the conversation until the real work reveals itself. They listen before the meeting, speak when it matters, and guide the modifications when scope must change. They don't reinforce what no longer serves the mission. They adjust the direction, hold the thread, and make sure the team keeps walking toward something that still holds meaning. Not every task is saved. Not every original promise makes the final cut. But purpose does. Purpose. That's what gets restored.

Without a shortcut, Hansel and Gretel found their way back, step by step, because they learned to see clearly, through illusion, through fear, and through the forest itself. The Apollo 13 crew didn't land on the Moon, but they did land. They made it home alive because the mission was redefined in time. That's the work of the project janitor. They don't defend the original plan at all costs, and they don't repeat the story the sponsor still hopes to tell. Instead, they keep sweeping until the path is visible again. They listen early, steady the team when it falters, and shift direction when the work demands it. Their focus is getting the project they inherited back to safety, even if the destination has changed.

Janitor's Keyring

When the mission changes, the project janitor doesn't turn off the pressure. They reroute the hose. They find a new path, set proper expectations, and bring the team home.

The Wisdom Within: Hansel and Gretel

The family had nothing left. No bread. No plan. Just two children and a forest deep enough to forget them in. The stepmother made the decision, and the father agreed. The children would be led into the woods and left behind.

There was no plan to find them again.

They wandered for days, cold, hungry, and lost, until they found a house in a clearing. The walls were made of cake. The windows were trimmed with sugar. It looked perfect. They broke off pieces and ate. That was when the door opened.

A woman smiled and welcomed them inside. She gave them food, a bed, and promises of safety.

She was a witch.

The next morning, Hansel woke in a cage. Gretel was handed a pot and told to cook. The witch planned to fatten the boy and eat him. That was her goal. Each day, she told Hansel to stretch out his finger so she could feel whether he had gained weight. He held out a bone, not finger. She couldn't tell.

Still, she grew impatient. "Fat or thin, I will eat him tomorrow."

She told Gretel to light the oven. When it was hot, she called her over.

"Lean in and check it," the witch said.

Gretel paused. "I don't know how."

It wasn't lack of knowledge. It was the beginning of a plan.

"Foolish girl," the witch said, and leaned in to show her.

Gretel didn't hesitate. She pushed the witch into the oven and shut the door. She freed her brother. Together, they searched the house and filled their pockets with what they could carry: gems, gold, anything that might help.

Then they left. Not back the way they came. There was no trail, no path to follow, nothing to return to. Ahead lay only a river, wide and cold, with no bridge, no boat, no clear way across. But a single white duck drifted near the bank. Hansel stepped forward first, and the duck carried him gently to the other side. Then it returned for Gretel. One crossed. Then the other. They didn't know where the river led, only that it moved forward.

And in time, without knowing exactly how, they found their way home.

When the plan disappears, keep moving. The trail back may be gone, but there is always a way.

-- Brothers Grimm, as told by a Project Janitor

Adding to Your Toolbox

Start with inspection: Before responding to dissatisfaction, revisit the original agreements. Review contracts, scope, decisions, and emails. Misalignment often hides in assumptions left unspoken.

Find the drift: Identify where expectations have strayed from current reality. Look for outdated milestones, deliverables that no longer apply, or requests still tied to a version of the project that no longer exists.

Clarify with context: Reframe gently. Don't argue. Show the difference between what was said and what was meant. Focus the conversation on shared definitions, not defensiveness.

Reset before the room: Have the conversation before the meeting. Surface concerns early. Ask what stakeholders believe is being delivered and why. Recalibrate while the pressure is low.

Influence without credit: Guide sponsors toward alignment without forcing it. Ask the right questions, show the right details, and let them arrive at the conclusion. Let them own the turn.

Reconfirm what was agreed: Don't assume alignment holds. Recap key decisions in plain language. Write them down. Follow up. Stakeholders often remember what they hoped to hear.

Stay close after consensus: Expect expectations to reappear. Watch for divergence from the plan in dashboards, emails, or hallway conversations. Reset as needed. Cleanup isn't one-and-done.

Walk the path forward: Even when the plan collapses, the mission can continue. Reroute calmly. Keep the team moving toward the goal that still matters, even if it's not the original one.

Chapter 5
Custodians of Communication: Clearing the Pipes

Executive Summary

Let's dive into communication cleanup. Issues rarely announce themselves. They slip in through polite agreement, vague updates, and the slow erosion of shared meaning. Chapter 5 explores how the project janitor spots these breakdowns before they become blowups. Rather than respond with a waving finger, the project janitor listens early, scrubs misalignment from routine conversations, and restores flow by reinforcing clarity through rhythm and presence. They steady the work with clear summaries, shared agreements, and the resolve to ask what others avoid. When handled with care, the project begins to move again because the message is finally clean enough to carry the weight. To start, here's the mess at hand.

The Mess at Hand

Most often, miscommunication starts with silence, the kind that clings to the corners of a video call, or pools in the space between emails where direction should live. You arrive mid-project, not to praise and unconditional support, but to the muffled hum of misalignment and likely inherent disfunction. One stakeholder thinks the milestone was due next Friday. Another didn't know there was a milestone at all. The team nods through the standup, eyes darting to inboxes, wondering what's been missed and who might be blamed for it. No one names the problem, but it slowly drips from every sentence like a slow leak behind the wall. This isn't just miscommunication. It's erosion. And the cleanup begins not with solutions, but with the courage to ask the question no one wants to speak aloud: What truth are we avoiding?

Silence doesn't stay quiet. It seeps into estimates, wraps itself around timelines, and hardens into assumptions. A requirement gets misread. A deadline drifts past, unnoticed. A team member nods along to avoid conflict, and the moment for clarification slips away. What began as a missing update becomes a misaligned sprint, a mistraced dependency, a mistrust. Then, by the time someone raises their voice, it's no longer about the issue but everything that came before it. The project janitor walks into this storm not with a sweeper, but with a question: When did we stop listening? Not just to each other but to the work itself. Because the mess doesn't shout. It echoes. And unless someone breaks the pattern, the echo will only get louder.

So, the team does what teams often do when clarity vanishes: they fill the silence with clatter. More meetings. More messages. More words that rarely say more. Agendas stretch. Threads multiply. Stories drag across sprints. Someone suggests a war room. Another war room. Someone else updates the slide deck, again. Yet beneath it all, the real issues remain untouched, buried under burndown charts and readiness spreadsheets, polished for optics instead of insight. The problem isn't that no one is speaking; it's that no one is connecting. The project janitor hears it in the rhythm: updates without direction, questions without response, answers that sound right but land hollow. It's a spit-shine on rust, masking a failure to communicate. And that's when the real cleanup begins.

Sometimes, the ones doing the most talking hold the least truth. The emperor walks the corridor in full regalia, and no one dares to say what's missing. The child hasn't spoken yet. Or maybe she's not in the room. Maybe she's standing at the edge of the project, reading the silence like blueprints and wondering when someone will admit that nothing fits. That's what Emily Roebling did. When her husband, the chief engineer of the Brooklyn Bridge project, fell ill and lost his voice, she became *his* bridge. She translated his technical instructions, soothed tempers, kept the work moving, and led through presence when no one expected her to lead at all. The city never gave her the title. But the bridge stands because she spoke when others wouldn't. Not every mess is loud, or obvious. Some wear medals. Some carry titles. But if no one's willing to name the gap, the collapse begins before the ribbon is ever cut. Speak up.

The Cleaning Strategy

Communication rarely begins with resonance. It begins with presence. The project janitor doesn't walk in to broadcast a message via megaphone; they arrive to receive. To observe. Why? Because beneath the filth of frustration is a trail of muddy prints leading to missed moments where someone could have clarified, could have realigned, but didn't. The strategy isn't to speak louder. It's to reconnect the lines that frayed the instant people started talking *past* one another instead of *to* one another. You can't fix a clogged line by shouting down the pipe. You do it by restoring the flow.

The project janitor listens differently. Not just to what's said, but to what keeps being repeated. What questions never get answered. What's phrased carefully to avoid accountability. Good communication isn't speech alone; it's pattern recognition. Because somewhere in the daily noise is the rattle of an overstuffed washer. Spinning. The circular conversation. The stakeholder who keeps asking the same thing three different ways. The team member who always agrees but never delivers. It'll be ready next week, again. Those rackety loops don't fix themselves. The project janitor doesn't just hear the noise; they chart the echo.

Remember the emperor with no clothes. He paraded forward, not because no one saw the problem, but because no one spoke. They whispered. They nodded. They repeated what they didn't believe to stay safe. The tailor didn't need magic. He only needed silence. Miscommunication thrives on consensus without clarity. The project janitor knows this pattern. Projects can go for months following a ritual of saying the right things, following the processes, yet delivering nothing. No one questions the spinning clatter. No one points out what's missing: the fabric, the raiment. Until the project janitor arrives. Not to embarrass. Not to blame. But to ask the question that breaks the echo. What are we *pretending* to understand?

The project janitor stops the cycle by carefully reintroducing the basic elements that healthy communication always carries. Messages must be clear and concise rather than coated in jargon or softened into meaninglessness. Listening must be active. Instead of waiting to speak, absorb what's being said, and what isn't. Openness isn't passive. Invite, reinforce, and protect it. Respect must be practiced before it is received, especially when tension rises. And mutual understanding must be verified, not assumed. The project janitor tracks these like early signs of a blockage breaking loose. A clarifying question that wasn't asked before. A teammate repeating back what they heard without being prompted. A pause before the reply. These are small things. But in a project clouded by polished talk and silent doubt, they're the first signs the noise is becoming a conversation.

Scrub Away the Chaos

There's no single fix for broken communication, but there is a way to start cleaning it up: scrub one surface at a time. The project janitor doesn't try to solve everything in one discussion. They start where most of the dust accumulates. A recurring meeting that leaves people more confused than when they entered. A stakeholder who dominates every call but says nothing new. A document that looks official but clarifies nothing. These aren't side issues. They're mold lodged in the tile grout.

The real work begins when the project janitor starts shaping how communication moves through the project. That doesn't necessarily mean adding meetings but changing the ones already on the calendar. Time becomes intentional. Questions are specific. Every conversation has a destination, and everyone in the room needs to know where. The project janitor identifies what isn't working such as calls that produce no decisions, reports with flash but no content, or bottleneck reports that hide real impediments. Either retool or remove the grime. Replace volume with clarity, habit with intent. Why? Because unchecked, dysfunctional communication doesn't just waste time, it erodes trust. And once that goes, the team stops listening, stops aligning, and starts protecting. You can't move a project forward when everyone's bracing for blame.

Scrubbing communication clean means making the unspoken visible. The project janitor might start with an updated RACI matrix (or something similar), a realignment of areas of responsibility: Who owns what? Who's responsible or accountable? Who's consulted (public) or confused (private)? Who's informed (public) or inconsequential (private)? Then come the working agreements. Are decisions made in the meeting or after it? Who has veto power? When do side conversations become blockers?

Next, introduce short summaries with all meeting notes and status reports. Just: What did we finish? What changed? What needs attention? Actions. Decisions. And when writing those updates, apply the BLOT principle - Bottom Line On Top. This method works for email as well. Say what matters first. Then explain. "We're behind on testing. Here's what we're doing." That's not just clear, it's janitorial. BLOT creates better communication, faster. It respects the recipient's time, sharpens decisions, and sweeps confusion out before it settles.

These tools cut through the grease. Because once communication has been restored, structure is what keeps it clean and clear. The project janitor isn't polishing what's broken. They're rebuilding the structure that keeps everything else from falling apart. Polish comes later.

With communication, you almost never start with a clean surface. Usually, you're handed a mess that doesn't listen - or worse, talks back. One noteworthy project cleanup began during a failing enterprise resource planning (ERP) system upgrade. The client PM, Mr. Shrinker, brought in midstream, had all the posture, title, tone, and talk, but none of the follow-through. He was buzzword sure. A self-proclaimed expert, he refused to use the collaborative ticketing system where every artifact lived. No project janitor, he skipped meetings, then sent emails demanding responses to questions that had already been asked and answered. When he did attend, he was polished. On the surface. In writing, sharp. He dismissed every recommendation with a smirk, then repeated the idea as his own two meetings later. He asked for clarity but dismissed it. He called documentation vague while refusing to read it.

On the vendor side, the PM injected after the first tapped out made all the difference. The project janitor didn't argue. He pointed to the record: tickets, notes, and contractual terms. He sent summaries with numbered responses and quiet accountability. When the requests crossed into out-of-scope territory, he redirected, firmly and without fanfare, back to the contract. Leadership was looped in only when necessary. The tone stayed professional. The message stayed consistent. Standard mop and bucket.

Progress didn't return with a major repair. It returned with structure. A meeting ran a half-hour shorter, giving back some desk time. A blocker was raised instead of buried. A real question landed without being followed by spin. There was no award. No ceremony. But the air had shifted. There was less friction, more connection. The team may not have noticed it, but the project janitor did. The drain cleared.

Of course, there was no time to linger. There were more chores, more hidden leaks behind other walls. Other places where the silence had started to echo a bit too loudly. There was a king to dress. The project wasn't yet clean, but it was no longer stuck. And sometimes, that's enough.

Lessons from the Janitor's Closet

Not every mess announces itself. Some just slide past inspection. That's what makes communication so difficult to clean. It's not a graph on a dashboard or a red-highlighted row in the tracker. It shows up as confusion with a smile. Agreement without alignment. Motion that feels like progress until someone double-checks what's actually been delivered.

The emperor didn't need to hypnotize anyone. He just needed a room full of people willing to keep walking without looking. The project janitor watches for that moment. The too-smooth meeting. The confident recap that leaves no room for questions. They don't wait for a breakdown. They step in while the floor still looks clean, because that's where the footprints start to show. The illusion may hold for a while, but the project janitor sees through it. Clarity is a clothed leader.

The project janitor doesn't fix communication by demanding it. They repair it the same way they fix everything else: by noticing what's out of alignment, what no longer fits, and what was never properly fastened in the first place. Most teams don't fall apart in the middle of a debate. They unravel slowly, under the weight of polite nods and half-stated agreements. The project janitor notices that weight. They hear it in agreements that skip clarification, in updates that sound impressive but answer nothing. They ask the question no one else will ask, not to poke, but to be sure the surface is worthy of the polish. They listen carefully to how people respond and to what they avoid. And when the pattern repeats, as it often does, they don't push harder. They adjust. They document what was said. They follow up with what was meant. They rewrite the meeting summary, holding it to the light just long enough for others to see the gaps. The project janitor is not the loudest voice in the room. They are the one who makes sure the room doesn't forget what was said. That's the lesson from the closet. Communication isn't just what you say. It's what you're willing to clarify, confirm, and return to until every dustmop in the room faces the same direction.

Keep your pressure washer ready for overconfident, acronym spewers, like Shrinker. They'll try to sell you the Brooklyn Bridge. And in some cases, they nearly do. The original chief engineer, John Roebling, died before construction could begin. His son, Washington, took over. He soon fell ill and became bedridden, unable to walk or speak clearly. The project stalled. The pressure mounted. Still, the bridge was too important to fail. Emily Roebling, Washington's wife, stepped in. She studied the math, learned the engineering, and managed the relationships. At one point, a politician attempted to take full credit for the bridge's progress and nearly convinced the public he was the reason it stood. But it wasn't his voice that carried the plan forward. It was hers. She translated blueprints into instructions, and those instructions into outcomes. Brick by brick, wire by wire, the bridge rose. Not because someone talked louder, or slicker, but because someone listened better. The project janitor didn't need the title. She carried the message. She kept it steady. That's what real communication looks like. Not noise. Not smoke. Not posture. Just clarity, earned, repeated, and anchored, until the structure holds.

Real communication is common sense applied with purpose. But in some rooms, common sense is as rare as a busy broom with all its bristles still straight. Shrinker will talk in spirals. Others will scribble mind maps, color-coded for chaos, and still can't name the last decision made. The project janitor brings something else entirely. They don't force agreement. They restore practicality. Not by speaking with extra volume, but by reducing the issue to its essence, clear, direct, remembered. They speak in full sentences. They ask real questions. They do the right things on time, in sequence, and without apology. Sometimes, the shine is as simple as asking, "What's the goal of this meeting?" and waiting long enough for someone to say it out loud. That's not heavy lifting. That's the art of common sense. You can't put it on a resume. But when it shows up in a project that's been drifting too long, everyone feels the change in momentum. The update has a point. The room breathes. The work realigns. And no one calls it leadership. But the project starts moving again. The mop leaves its mark. The bridge gets built.

Spills and Cleanups

The breakdown of communication rarely begins in chaos. It begins in comfort. Rather than asking the question, a misunderstood point slips under the rug. No one notices the skipped recap or the meeting summary that sounds evergreen clean but avoids what no one wanted to say aloud. That's how the spill starts, not with a scream, but with silence disguised as agreement. A failure of common sense. And by the time the truth surfaces, it's not a puddle. It's a pool of sludge. Soaked into the schedule. Baked into the budget. Tangled into the backlog. The project janitor doesn't panic. They trace just far enough to stop the pattern. They look for where the drip began, then set blame aside. Because until someone sees the source, the floor stays wet. But once the shape is known, the cleanup takes hold. We don't rewind. We realign. All that matters now is what we say next.

Most communication spills don't need confrontation. They need containment. The project janitor doesn't storm the meeting. They quiet it. Not with silence, but with sequence. First, they clarify what was said. Then what was heard. Then what was left to dry between the lines. They ask for confirmation, not concession. They reread the action items. They refocus the summary. Not to prove a point, but to find the point that got lost. Because when communication fails, people don't just mishear. They protect. They posture. They remember what happened to match what they hoped to hear. And by the time the blame has been preloaded into the conversation, it takes more than correction to reset the tone. That's when the project janitor moves carefully, rinsing the exchange, restating the goal, and handing the keys back to the team, not to start over, but to start clean.

One of the loudest messes came not from failure, but from frustration. With Shrinker's leadership fraying, the executive lit into the team on a particularly tense status call. Voice raised. Accusations flying. She called the analysis phase plan a disaster, the communication broken, vendor leadership absent. And she wasn't wrong about everything. But her delivery was hot coffee, spilled hard across the boardroom table. The project janitor didn't match the tone. He didn't flinch. He let her finish. Then he thanked her for raising the concerns and offered a short summary of the issue at hand. Just the facts. What had drifted. What had been promised. What had been missed. He offered to send a recap with clear action items by the end of the day. And he did. Numbered. Neutral. Precise. He looped in the sponsor quietly. Not to escalate, but to steady the wheel. The next meeting was calmer. Not warm, but calmer. The work resumed. The yelling didn't return. Because what the client really needed wasn't a fight. It was to feel heard, and to walk away with something strong enough to defend. And that's what the project janitor delivered. Not a rebuttal. Not a retort. Just enough clarity to wipe up the coffee and keep the project moving.

The single biggest problem in communication,
is the illusion that it has taken place.
-- George Bernard Shaw

Adding the Polish

Clean communication doesn't maintain itself. Even after the coffee's been wiped, the deliverable rewritten, the meeting calmed, there's still dust. Always accumulating. The slow return of shortcuts that never quite worked. Secret priority lists. Undocumented decisions. That's why the project janitor doesn't walk away when the tension fades. They stay and listen to how the language reforms. How questions evolve. Whether clarity holds or needs another rinse. The polish isn't for optics. It's for durability. Because one hard conversation doesn't fix a culture. One clean status report doesn't fix the habit of nodding instead of asking. If the team only speaks clearly during crisis, they haven't learned to communicate, they've just learned to brace. The polish is what transforms recovery into routine. A rhythm of updates that control clarity. Agendas that move. Summaries that reflect what was actually said, not just what looked good on a slide.

The project janitor reinforces that pattern, not only with rules, but with example. They show what clarity looks like. What it sounds like. How it feels when someone asks a question not to challenge, but to align. They reinforce the positive. They protect the space. Because when communication works, it stops being a defense. It becomes a bridge. Built line by line. Maintained with care. And when it holds - when someone raises their voice, not in frustration but in purpose - that's how you know the message is clean. That's how it happened in Brooklyn.

Janitor's Keyring

Proper communication doesn't maintain itself. It drifts. It dulls. It fills until it's clogged. The project janitor keeps the pipes clear by listening early, rinsing often, and speaking up to sweep the path ahead.

The Wisdom Within: The Emperor's New Clothes

There once was a leader who prized image above all else. Progress, productivity, success, he wanted the world to see it before it was even real. So, when two weavers arrived in the kingdom promising to craft the finest clothes imaginable, garments so refined, they would be invisible to anyone unworthy or incompetent, the emperor hired them without hesitation. He needed to be seen in something exceptional. Something no one else could wear.

The weavers set to work on empty looms. They demanded gold and silk, praised the pattern, and asked for quiet while they created. And though nothing ever appeared, no one dared to question it. Ministers came to inspect the work, saw nothing, and said everything. They feared what it would mean if they admitted the truth. So, they nodded. They smiled. They praised the weave and returned to the court with glowing reports.

Eventually, the emperor himself went to view the fabric. He, too, saw nothing, but he was not about to confess that. So, he praised the colors. Admired the cut. And when the day came for the procession, he put on the invisible robes, held his head high, and walked through the capital.

The crowd, already primed with praise and fear, played along. They clapped. They bowed. They admired. All except one child, who had not yet learned how to lie. The child pointed, confused, and said the thing everyone else had buried.

He isn't wearing anything.

The words broke the spell. One by one, the crowd looked again. The illusion collapsed, not because the lie changed, but because someone said it aloud. Identified it.

The project janitor knows this moment. Meetings filled with nods, updates that circle, praise without substance. Projects where the process is honored, but the truth is missing. The project janitor doesn't shout. They don't embarrass. But they ask the question no one else will: "Is this working?" And if the answer is absent, they look closer. They point to what's missing, not to humiliate, but to restore what's real. Because clarity doesn't arrive through fear. It arrives through courage. And when it does, the work finally begins to wear something honest.
-- Hans Christian Andersen, as told by a Project Janitor

Adding to Your Toolbox

Start by listening: Before jumping in, observe how the team communicates. Listen to what's said, what's avoided, and what keeps repeating. Silence reveals more than noise.

Ask the question no one wants to ask: When progress feels off, but no one can explain why, surface the unspoken. Ask what's unclear. Point gently to what's missing.

Interrupt the echo: Look for circular updates, vague language, or updates that sound clean but clarify nothing. Stop the spin by asking for specifics.

Realign the routine: Identify recurring meetings, reports, or conversations that confuse more than clarify. Reset them with a clear purpose and defined outcomes.

Make clarity visible: Don't rely on memory or shared interpretation. Recap action items and decisions in writing. Use plain language and keep it brief.

Apply structure to updates: Introduce short summaries using BLOT (Bottom Line On Top). Start with what matters, then explain. Respect attention spans.

Rebuild accountability: Revisit who owns what. Clarify roles, responsibilities, and escalation paths. When confusion persists, refine working agreements.

Stay calm when tension rises: If someone escalates, don't match their tone. Let them speak. Then respond with a short, clear summary of facts and next steps.

Repeat when needed: Even after things are reset, expect drift. Check how people refer to the plan, how meetings are run, and whether clarity holds.

Maintain the rhythm: Good communication isn't a one-time fix. Keep reinforcing what clear sounds like, how it moves, and where it lands. Restore the rhythm until it holds.

Chapter 6
Stocking the Closet: Resources and Tools to Tackle Disorder

Executive Summary

Tools alone don't solve chaos. In every midstream project, there's a moment when effort stops working, when the team needs more than motion. They need a reliable system. Reliable resources and tools. Chapter 6 explores how the project janitor restocks the closet, not with whatever tools are lying around, but with what the work really demands.

This chapter begins with a fable, reminding us that the spinning wheel isn't the problem, it's the secrecy around it. Cleanup begins the moment someone identifies the cost. From there, we walk through the real-world story of a satellite receiver project where clarity replaced crisis, not through force, but by equipping the team with tools that matched the task.

Let's spin back to 1666.

The Mess at Hand

It started with a spark, a fire on Pudding Lane, and by morning, the city was ash. London didn't burn clean. It blistered. It buckled. It collapsed under the weight of its own density. By sunrise, cathedral domes were charcoal, homes were cinders, and the great guildhalls of trade and craft stood only as smoke-stained ghosts. The air reeked of soot and silence.

But what followed was worse than flame: the aftermath.

Cleanup began not with coordination, but with confusion. Competing visions. Conflicting surveys. Rebuilds drawn atop ruins before the stone had cooled. Brick met marble met bureaucracy. Every craftsman arrived with their own design and none with the same plan. Or even the same ideas. The fire had cleared the map, but no one could agree what belonged on it.

Then came Sir Christopher Wren.

He didn't posture. He observed. He walked the footprint of the fallen city not only to grieve, but to measure. Where others traced monuments, he traced the pattern beneath them. He carried not declarations but tools: compass, caliper, slate. While ambition circled around him, he drew quiet, disciplined lines within. And from the turmoil, he laid out what could endure. It may not have been the final solution. Still, it was a foundation.

The cleanup always begins with what the fire leaves behind. A half-finished project. A gutted backlog. A borrowed team and an overeager plan. Schedules are scattered across drive folders. Some are secrets. Tools lie tattered from disuse. Each meeting opens with a greeting and closes with confusion. Everyone is working. Still, is anyone aligned?

The virtual broom closet is open, yet it's cluttered with what others forgot to carry out. Diagrams from past initiatives. Project files meant for tools that no longer load. Templates written for a different style, a different year, a different kind of mess. Bottles are mislabeled. Mops lean dry against cracked tile. And somewhere, a voice asks for velocity, louder this time. Always louder.

This is disorder. Misalignment long uncorrected. The structure hollowed out by updates that never landed, responsibilities that changed without redefinition, resources stretched across timelines that no longer fit.

And now the mess is yours because the original plan failed to evolve. The closet wasn't stocked. The shelves were never checked. The supplies went stale. And now the project runs thin, under-resourced, over-promised, and expected to arrive intact.

This is where the project janitor begins. As Wren did, we dive in with gloved hands. Not by redrawing the skyline in a single sweep, but by stocking the tools, rebuilding the map, and restoring the rhythm beneath the rubble. One system at a time. One step at a time. Until something stable returns. Order. Durable enough to stand.

The modern mess doesn't rise in smoke, but in apathy. A repository full of misnamed files. Project logs that haven't been touched since kickoff. Teams assigned but split across three other initiatives. Maybe more than three. The closet swings open, and what's inside doesn't match the work ahead. A few templates. A process map from last year. A task tracker no one updates. The structure failed because no one checked the shelves, chose the proper tools, or was trained to use them. The cleanup starts by setting aside the grail of completion and asking how to retool the closet.

The Cleaning Strategy

Some messes are deeply woven into the job description. A promise was made that must be delivered. A timeline was shared. A scope was accepted without checking the thread count. Then a fire broke out. Now, the team is staring at a pile of straw, expected to turn it into something that shines. But straw doesn't shine, does it?

When the purpose surfaces, the project janitor does not spin into panic. They don't bluff. They don't fake it. They take stock. Before any more work begins, they reach for the closet, not for a magic eraser, but for a method. Because when leadership expects gold, the first task isn't to deliver. It's to determine whether the wheel, the room, and the raw materials can even support a single turn of the spinning wheel.

The strategy begins with one move: rebuild the system that supports the work. Not the final product. Not the milestones. The system. The team, the timeline, the tools. The missing conversations. The definitions that haven't been agreed to. The supplies that never arrived.

Projects don't end up needing a project janitor because no one tried. They get there because something essential was overlooked. Take stock. The closet must be re-evaluated. Forget how full it looks. The real question is whether what's in it matches what the job really requires. That's where the real cleanup begins.

No one restocks a janitor's closet without first opening the door and counting what's inside. Observation starts the journey. Quiet, steady, and thorough. The project janitor doesn't rush to assignments or dashboards. First, they walk the floor. They attend the meetings. They read the documentation, not for polish, but for pattern. If the bottleneck report hasn't been updated, the sprint icebox is stale, or the estimates don't match the work in motion, the gaps will surface. Before any tool is added or reassigned, the project janitor watches how the work flows, or perhaps more importantly, where it doesn't.

Most closets contain more than what's needed. So do most projects. A dozen tracking tools, none consistently updated. Many unused since the Carter administration, collecting dust. A shared drive cluttered with folders named for janitors from the past. Software in boxes that only run from floppies. Conference phones neatly cord-wrapped and stashed in the corner. Agenda templates in monochrome. Roles assigned but never realigned. Meetings that generate motion but not momentum. The project janitor doesn't assume that every item stored for use is still serving the work. Some tools were introduced in a panic. Others were inherited without question. Some are just relics: familiar, but untested. Before anything is thrown out, the project janitor identifies the useful, what is being bypassed, and what is getting in the way.

Next, the project janitor doesn't just tidy. They restructure. They redraw calendars to reflect true availability, not wishful allocation. They unearth blocked hours hidden behind recurring phantom invites, clutter from projects past, and clear them out. They archive outdated kanban boards and select a single intake system, regardless of the platform, so new work stops sneaking in through hallway conversations or instant message dings. They recraft burndown charts to show actual hours worked, not the ideal. They realign timeboxes to match deliverables and confirm fresh due dates with leadership. The team stops spinning in every direction and starts building in one. The project janitor leads every decision with two questions. First, does this setup help the team complete real work at the pace this project now demands? Then, are we positioned to satisfy our sponsor? Note the order. Without the first, the second never happens.

Let's return to the Brothers Grimm. The miller's daughter never asked for the task. Yet there she stood, locked in a room with a pile of dull, lifeless straw, expected to spin it into gold before sunrise. No help. No tools. Merely an ultimatum. The magic arrives, yes, but only with a cost. That's the danger of the wrong setup: a project built on panic trades real planning for invisible debts. The project janitor doesn't play that game. They don't promise to spin all night while others sleep. Instead, they match the work to the people and the people to the work. Not everyone spins. Not everyone should. But every hand must land where it brings value.

Stocking the closet is more than tools alone. It's about people. The project janitor looks past the org chart and sees what's really in motion. Who's already overloaded. Who's in the wrong seat. Who's underused. Sometimes, it's who needs to take his stapler to the basement. Delegation isn't a handoff. It's an alignment. The janitor matches talent to task, not title to role. A strong communicator takes the stakeholder calls. A detail-minded analyst handles the defect logs. The person who keeps asking the right questions might just be the ideal scrum master. No janitor's closet works unless what's stored there is placed in the hands of the right person.

Scrub Away the Chaos

Ambiguity is where panic hides. The project janitor identifies and labels it. Who owns the backlog? What defines done? How do we weave the straw of the many systems of record into a cohesive project status report? Every shadow in the workflow becomes a hiding place for risk. In the fairy tale, the spinning wheel only seemed magical. Its power didn't lie in the tool, but in the secret, from a promise forced out of fear. The spell broke the moment the name was spoken. Speak it. In a project, the same rule applies. When ownership is clear and responsibilities are named aloud, the illusion ends. Once roles, priorities, and expectations are clearly named, the work begins to obey the plan.

Recognition is the start of the scrub. Once roles begin to take shape and expectations surface, the project janitor moves to close the loops. They find the leaks. They follow missed handoffs to the source. They trace incomplete action items to the meetings where they were assigned, and to whom. They cross-check status reports against what's been delivered. No assumption is left unverified. Repeated impediments, missing approvals, gaps between estimates and outcomes are labeled, logged, and addressed in sequence. They clarify the documentation. This isn't policy. It's pattern repair. The scrubbing continues until every conversation reflects the structure beneath it.

Rumpelstiltskin. We said it. Now, the spinning slows. The panic quiets. What once was ruled by apparent magic now begins to look like real process. The straw is sorted. The room is swept. The team moves with clarity, not constraint. Tasks no longer pile up in corners, unclaimed. Assignments are named, tracked, and owned. Reports match reality. Estimates reflect the hands that will do the work. The project janitor doesn't promise gold by morning. They restore a system where effort yields value: without fear, and without tricks.

Lessons from the Janitor's Closet

In a satellite receiver manufacturing plant just outside Boston, the work had already begun to unravel. The order was big, 360 systems for a prominent client from Fenway, and the pressure was building. Shipments arrived late, and many key pieces were missing. Assemblers were overworked and frustrated. Benches and storage looked like a garage sale in a nor'easter. Boxes were mislabeled, most not labeled at all. Some materials arrived damaged, others couldn't be found when needed. Mismatched tools. Confused people. A timeline that had already floated down the Charles. Deadlines came closer. The trucks were on their way. That's when Tom Reid walked in. No entourage. No blame. Just a project janitor with a notebook, a quiet presence, and a reputation for cleaning up chaos without making more of it. He didn't lecture. He watched. He asked a few questions. Then he walked the floor again, more slowly this time. The real work had not yet begun. But already, the energy had reset.

Tom didn't start with more meetings. He started with more movement. He spent the first day sweeping from assembly station to assembly station, talking to technicians, noting which tasks were flowing and which ones stalled. He watched people wait for tools that never returned, for parts that were probably there, if only to be found. He saw materials rerouted without documentation, let alone approval. No two assemblers followed the same build sequence. Some were doing three jobs. Some were doing none. At the end of the day, he found a quiet corner and made a list. Not a plan. Not yet. A list of what was broken and what might still be usable. The cleanup wouldn't start with speeches and slide decks. It would start with the floor.

The next day, he spun the list into action. Tom worked with HR to bring in a short-term labor crew. Not consultants. Extra hands. He rebalanced the workload so that no assembler got buried, and no one stood idle. He walked the storage area with two line workers and a clipboard. Together, they relabeled every box. Damaged parts were pulled and flagged for return. A simple inventory sheet went up on the wall with a sharpie and a promise: "This stays current." By noon, teams were finding what they needed in minutes instead of hours. No speeches. No dashboards. Just order. Restored one shelf and one shift at a time. Still, 360 units to go.

When it came time for the final push, Tom didn't call it overtime. He called it the Assembly Day Workshop. It wasn't a slogan. It was a signal. Food showed up. Zeppelin played low in the background. Not too low. Tom didn't point or bark. He built. He stood beside the team, tightening brackets, answering questions, moving product down the line. Not faster but steadier. Energy returned, not from pressure, but from presence. And somehow, across a single long night, straw turned to gold. The last unit boxed to ship just as the first rays of sunlight reached the loading dock.

The client never saw the cleanup. They saw a delivery, on time, fully packed, flawless in quality and appearance. Still, inside the plant, something more important shined. Teams that once worked in silos now shared a common cadence. The janitor's closet, restocked, held not theory but tools to match the mess: a right-sized crew, a shared system, a plan that fit the work instead of forcing it. What Tom left behind wasn't just a clean floor. It was a better layout. A working flow. And a team that no longer mistook panic for progress. The satellite receivers rolled out in neat rows, but the real signal was clear. Order had been restored.

Spills and Cleanups

When leaders treat the janitor's closet like a junk drawer, grabbing whatever's there and pushing forward, the result is rarely effective. Not every resource is a fit for the job. Not every tool can turn a screw. Tools and resources must be aligned with proper use cases. Handing out improper tools to the wrong people is like taping blueprints to a broom and expecting an architect. Everyone works harder. Nothing gets fixed. The team gets flooded with new tasks, new trackers, new urgency. But no clarity. No fit. No rhythm. The mess isn't cleaned. It's compacted. The project janitor knows better. They sharpen the tools. They prep the surface. They clean with care, not wasted motion.

A tidy closet doesn't guarantee delivery, but a cluttered one almost always causes delay. Teams reach for the wrong tools not because they work, but because they feel familiar. Spreadsheets pose as systems of record. Slide decks stand in for real plans. Email threads carry decisions that never reach the team. These tools aren't broken, but misused. The project janitor doesn't toss them out. They streamline. One tracker replaces five. A shared intake form replaces hallway conversations, email nudges, and Teams pings. No more requests lost in passing or updates whispered without record. The intake system becomes the front door to the work: visible, standard, and owned. Status lives where everyone can find it. Approvals land on the signature line. Roadmaps, workflows, and reports stop gathering dust and start supporting progress. The project janitor restores the closet to fit the work. Every tool matches a task. Every task fits the plan. And every hand wears a fitted glove. Transparency removes disorder.

Give me six hours to chop down a tree,
and I will spend the first four sharpening the axe.
-- Abraham Lincoln

Adding the Polish

Wren didn't rebuild London overnight. He redrew the lines, set the stones, and stepped back. The system he restored wasn't measured by speed. It was measured by endurance. The footprint he left behind wasn't loud. It was organized. Deliberate. Designed for others to walk, not just admire. The project janitor thinks the same way. The last task isn't to finish the job. It's to make sure the work can continue without falling apart. The closet stays stocked. The tools stay visible. The team knows how to clean without waiting for permission. That's the polish. Not perfection. Sustainability.

The project janitor brings more than a fixed chart or a clean board. They bring rhythm. They show what alignment looks like. What it feels like when a tool fits the task. When the intake system captures the chaos before it hits the floor. They reinforce what works. They protect what flows. Because when structure holds, it invites the team to hold it too. Not with ceremony, but with ownership. A well-stocked closet isn't a showpiece. It's a system built to carry weight, day after day. That's how you know the assembly line is sound. London's calling.

Janitor's Keyring

Don't just grab what's left in the closet. Stock it with what the work will require, before disorder makes the choice for you.

The Wisdom Within: Rumpelstilt-project

Once, in a small kingdom where promises carried more weight than plans, a miller told the king his daughter could spin straw into gold. She couldn't. But the king liked the sound of it. So he locked her in a room with a pile of straw, a spinning wheel, and an expectation: gold by morning.

No help. No tools. Just a door that closed behind her.

She wept. She panicked. And then he appeared. Not the king. The little man with a grin too wide. And for his services, a price too vague. He asked for a necklace. She gave it. He spun the straw into gold. The next night, another room. Another pile. Another deal. She gave a ring.

And on the third night, with nothing left to offer, she promised him her firstborn child. The very little man said yes. He spun. The gold gleamed.

But the debt remained.

She pleaded for a release, a way out of the mess. The little man, toying, gave her a riddle. Guess his name, and the debt would vanish.

She tried everything. Bartholomew. Horace. Gideon. Names from stories. Names from dreams. None were right. With each failure, the room grew heavier. She paced, she cried, and still the wheel sat in the corner, silent now, but full of threat.

On the final night, when the time came to collect, he returned. Laughing. Certain she would never guess his name. But someone had heard him in the woods, dancing around a fire, singing it aloud.

She said it.

And the magic lost its grip.

The promise ended not with another trade, but with a word. Not more work. More clarity.

Every project janitor has their Rumpelstilt-project moment. A deal struck too fast. A promise made under pressure. A shortcut buried in the backlog and passed off as a system. The spinning wheel isn't the problem. The secrecy is. The mess begins when no one names the cost. But the cleanup begins the moment someone does. That's when the straw becomes gold.
-- Brothers Grimm, as told by a Project Janitor

Adding to Your Toolbox

Observe the real workflow: Before you stock anything, watch how the work is actually being done. Sit in meetings, walk the floor, and ask quiet questions. Do not fix what you haven't seen.

Take honest inventory: Open the closet. Count what is there. Identify what tools are active, outdated, duplicated, or missing. Label them clearly.

Clear out the clutter: Remove templates, trackers, and systems that no longer support the team. If a tool is ignored or patched over, let it go.

Rebuild the support system: Reset calendars to reflect real availability. Archive old boards. Define a single intake path. Make work visible and trackable again.

Realign ownership: Confirm who owns what. Do not assume. Match responsibility to individuals, not titles. Clarify any handoffs or overlaps.

Match tools to the actual task: Every tool must serve a clear purpose. If it does not help the team complete real work at the pace required, replace it.

Match people to the work: Observe strengths. Assign based on ability, not hierarchy. Align skilled hands to where they bring value.

Name what has been avoided: Call out gaps in process, undefined roles, and silent blockers. Panic thrives where responsibilities go unnamed.

Tighten the rhythm: Once the system is restocked, reinforce the structure. Monitor the flow of new work. Check that assignments stick. Adjust as needed.

Make it sustainable: Leave behind a system the team can maintain. Teach them how to restock, reset, and respond without relying on you to return.

Chapter 7
The Overflowing Bucket: Managing Risks and Spills

Executive Summary

Risk doesn't always roar. Sometimes it drips, stalls, or whispers, until the system gives way all at once. This chapter explores how overlooked signals become floods, and how the project janitor responds when the weight finally causes a spill. Drawing lessons from Pompeii's collapse and a modern manufacturing meltdown, we explore what happens when risk registers gather dust and warning signs go ignored. The result is never sudden. It only looks that way in hindsight.

The project janitor doesn't prevent every spill. They inherit the aftermath. Their role is not to panic, but to contain. Not to blame, but to restore. Using structure as the anchor, they steady the team, reactivate stalled systems, and rebuild trust through visible progress. Through the lens of Stone Soup, we see that risk recovery starts not with control, but with invitation. One structure. One cleared space. One steady hand at the pot. That's how risks stop spreading and how restoration begins.

The Mess at Hand

It started with a vibration. Then annoying tremors. The expected kind of disturbance people learned to ignore. A nuisance. The kind that rattled clay pottery, cracked through walls of stone, and gave the town something to talk about. In Pompeii, the warning signs came early, many years early. The mountain rumbled. Ash rose. Wells went dry. Still, the shops stayed open. The temples rang their bells. People patched the columns, painted their frescos, and took no note. Because that's what people do when the weight doesn't shift all at once. Is everyone okay? Great. They wait for a reason to act. And then the skies open.

It happened. Not a flicker or another warning bell, but an end. First, the mountain cracked. A scream of earth. Heat. Smoke. Crisis. The kind of collapse that leaves no time for strategy, only reaction. People ran. Some froze. Some turned back for what they thought they could save. By then, the system had already failed. Streets vanished. Roofs caved. The air thickened into ash. Entire households buried mid-meal, tools still in hand, tasks unfinished. Time turned molten. People to stone. Pompeii didn't fall because of surprise. It fell because no one believed they needed to act. Risk doesn't roar at first. It whispers. It settles into routine. It waits for the moment when no one's watching. Pompeii fell because no one moved while there was still time to move.

Projects don't erupt. They send signals. First a vibration. Stalled backlog. Then tremors begin: missed deadlines, rising defect counts, updates that feel more hopeful than honest. Alerts get silenced because they're inconvenient. The risk register goes stale. A risk gets logged but never owned. Another gets flagged but no one follows up. Then one day, a contract gets missed, a release rolls out broken, a stakeholder walks out of the room. And the power's already down. The data is gone. All risks have been realized. By the time the spill is noticed, the whole thing feels like lava: fast, hot, and irreversible. The end. Or is it?

This is where the project janitor steps in. Armed not with blame or with drama. The eruption has already happened. The worst is in the rubble. Their job is to understand the shape of the damage and begin to restore order. They ask where the risk register is, when it was last updated, and who owns it now. They check the intake system, the system of record, if it exists. They walk the floor, visiting one stakeholder at a time to see what's really in motion. And what's in ashes. They look for patterns. For quiet signals that were missed or ignored. The mess has happened. All that matters now is what we do next.

The Cleaning Strategy

The cleanup starts with purposeful containment. The project janitor doesn't rush in with resolutions. They focus on stopping the spread of lava. First, they halt any work that adds to the damage. And any commotion that adds to the drama. They pause deliverables tied to unresolved risks. They freeze status reporting to avoid recycling bad information. They suspend new change orders until someone maps the leaks and seals them. Some meetings may move. After all, no one mops a floor still covered in rubble. Protect the project. Preserve what's left. Containment gives the team room to breathe. It draws a clear line around the mess so the real cleanup can begin.

Then we stabilize. The project janitor doesn't eliminate risk. Risk lives everywhere. Still, they steady the environment so the team can see it clearly. That begins with communication, one conversation at a time. They ask the right questions. What's still true? What's already gone? Who feels it, and who doesn't yet know it? They rebuild rhythm by returning to documented process. If no documentation exists, they write it. They reopen the risk register and revalidate it. What can we mitigate? How? They restore client-vendor communication through a single, visible system of record. No surprises. No hallway requests. Stabilization doesn't mean everything is under control. It means everything is visible. And from visibility, control becomes possible.

The rubble is before us. We breathe it in. We exhale it. We've marked the edge, contained it. We've identified what's missing, stabilized it. Now is the moment most teams freeze as they wait for a return to normal, a fix, a plan - a savior. But such a cleanup cannot jump the line. Normal doesn't begin without structure. It begins with a single pot. That's how the story of Stone Soup begins. Not with abundance, but with arrangement. One person sets the center. They light the fire. They place the pot. And slowly, others come forward, not because they were told to, but because something steady invited them in. The project janitor doesn't bring the soup. They bring the structure others use to cook and serve it.

Structure is what invites contribution. It gives progress somewhere to land and something to hold onto. Without it, even the best intentions evaporate. The project janitor asks for solutions without expectation, only to understand what risks remain and how to wrap structure around them. They clear space. They set the frame. They make it safe to add without making things worse. Once that frame exists, risk stops spreading. The team stops spinning. And the result is a restored system, clean, grounded, and ready to move.

Scrub Away the Chaos

The traditional tale *Stone Soup* doesn't begin with rescue. It begins with structure. The village is tired. The people are scattered. No one sees a way forward. But one traveler brings a pot, places it at the center, and sets the fire. The visitor doesn't demand help. They don't demand trust. They build something solid, visible, and calm. And others respond.

That's how the project janitor begins to scrub. The project still carries risk. Trust may still be fractured. But now there's at least a frame. The project janitor doesn't mop in circles. They move with intention. One task. One category. One risk at a time. They start with the simplest: what can be removed? What no longer applies? What's been duplicated? Then they look for rot, anything that pretends to be structure but quietly adds risk. Unused tools. Stale reports. Legacy estimates no one believes. Each removal clears the surface. Each decision steadies the room.

The first step in scrubbing risk is recognition. The project janitor gathers the list. Not just the formal register, if one exists, but the verbal warnings, the whispered concerns, the patterns in meeting notes and status calls. Then they sort. Prioritize. What's already happened. What's likely to happen. What can be ignored. What can't. The categories aren't complicated, they're clear. Impact. Likelihood. Ownership. Action. Not every risk needs attention today, but every risk needs a place. Without categorization, every threat feels urgent. And when everything is urgent, and resources overwhelmed, nothing gets cleaned.

Once the risks are sorted, the project janitor looks for momentum. Not in speeches or dashboards, but in small, visible wins. A teammate resolves a broken dependency. A vendor shows up on time. A blocked task finally moves. The scrum team finishes all their stories in one sprint. These aren't miracles. They're decisions. When risk clouds a project with ash, confidence fades. Early wins return proof. Progress not promises. A sign that structure in motion has moved the crumbled stone. And each small fix sends a message: we're not done, but we're moving.

The project janitor scrubs with a list and a plan. They assign every risk that sits unclaimed. They replace vague estimates with collaboratively agreed numbers. They document blockers and keep them from drifting through meetings. They don't fix everything. Still, they identify what's real and outline what's next. They make visibility the working surface. Every action lands in a shared space the team can track.

Stone soup. The fable hits the mark. One ladle at a time, one ingredient at a time. The pot doesn't boil because of urgency; it boils because someone keeps the fire steady. That's how projects recover: one decision, one task, one cleaned surface at a time.

The cleanup never looks impressive while it's happening. But that's the point. When it works, it feels simple. Quiet. Ordinary. The mess shrinks. The team steadies. The weight redistributes. Not because someone saved the project, but because someone stocked the pot, stirred what mattered, and cleared just enough space for progress to return. And sometimes, that's all it takes to turn an impossible recovery into something solid again. That's how it happened at Maple Creamery.

Lessons from the Janitor's Closet

They made the best ice cream in the country. That's what the sign said: Maple Creamery, proud, award-winning, best. It was the kind of place that felt more a manufacturing facility. For the locals, they hand-packed quarts, crafted frozen cakes, and smiled when you called them nostalgic. But behind the freezer doors, charm gave way to oversight.

The frozen dessert division had expanded fast, with a warehouse wall lined with new walk-in freezers, a state-of-the-art conveyor, and a modern alert system wired to the plant manager's phone. Yet the risk register sat blank. The backup power plan remained "under review." No one in operations, leadership, or even with the vendor had followed the alert wire all the way back to the breaker panel.

The factory ran fine for eight months. No alerts necessary. Then came the Fourth of July. A contractor, working on a long-overdue service ticket, flipped the wrong breaker. Freezers three through seven went dark. There was no backup power. No real-time alert. Only silence. The mountain had erupted.

Incredibly, two hundred and fifty pallets of product, from fudge swirl to mango sorbet to pistachio crumble, had melted into memory, slowly and finally, like a lava flow. They couldn't save a single bucket. They destroyed months of effort, then spent the rest of the year chasing losses, laying off staff, and reprinting brochures without the word *best*.

Someone had logged the risk once, early during installation: "Power loss = spoil risk." But no one claimed it. No one built a plan. No one checked it twice. Five freezers failed, and no one knew the risk had been realized.

That's the lesson. Risks don't always erupt. Sometimes they melt. One missed update. One neglected wire. One system everybody skips because it "usually works." That's all it takes for the lava to hit the fan. A project janitor walks the plant differently. They ask what changed, what failed, and who last checked the system meant to catch it. They assess the risk, not just record it. Because containment is about identifying the boundary. Stabilization doesn't mean calm. It means clarity, visibility. Cleanup doesn't have to start with a legion of shop vacs, but with a review of structure, ownership, and everything the team assumed someone else was watching.

The project janitor walks away with more than a list. They walk away knowing what held, what cracked, and what got missed when no one was looking. Recovery has a rhythm. Contain the spill before you promise a fix. Stabilize the system before you share a timeline. Categorize and assess risks before they escalate. Scrub what needs scrubbing, especially the parts no one else wants to touch. Find what's missing without assuming someone else checked the line.

Because risk doesn't disappear. But when the structure holds and the team sees clearly, risk becomes manageable, something the project can carry, one mitigation at a time.

Spills and Cleanups

The greatest risk in a midstream project isn't what no one sees, it's what everyone sees, and no one addresses. Desensitized to the sounds, the team logs the risk but never owns it. Flagged but not escalated. Known but not prioritized. Everyone assumes someone else is watching. But no one is.

So risk grows, quietly, until it melts or erupts.

The project janitor doesn't inherit the unknown. They inherit the ignored. And the ignored is harder to contain, harder to stabilize. The cleanup doesn't begin with discovery but with disappointment. The moment when the team realizes the mess wasn't a surprise. It was just easier to disregard the signs. Until it was too late.

The weight of a project rarely comes from a single event. It builds slowly: one delay, one assumption, one missed opportunity to speak up. The failure rarely feels dramatic in the moment. It feels normal. Until something breaks. And by then, it's too late for the nail to save the kingdom.

For want of a nail the shoe was lost.
For want of a shoe the horse was lost.
For want of a horse the rider was lost.
For want of a rider the battle was lost.
For want of a battle the kingdom was lost.
And all for the want of a horseshoe nail.
-- Benjamin Franklin

Adding the Polish

Pompeii failed not only because the mountain erupted. It failed because no one moved while they still could. The signs were there. The ground shook. The wells dried. The sky changed. But the city carried on as if weight would wait.

The project janitor doesn't stand in ash to mourn. They stand there to see. They read the patterns beneath the ruins. They ask who owned the warning, what went unanswered, and how the system responded when the pressure rose. They contain, stabilize, and restore structure.

Polish is sparkle, but only where structure holds. It doesn't cover the cracks; it exposes what's sound and what isn't. It brings clarity. It brings consistency. It allows the team to move forward without stepping back into the same mess. Once structure returns, rhythm follows. The team updates the risk register. They keep the system of record alive. They learn what risk looks like, and they keep their eye on the signs. They mitigate those they must. Plans B and C are designed ahead of disaster. They find opportunities. They accept the risks they can. The project may carry scars, but it stands because someone watched and kept it stable.

That's the polish. Not a perfect plan. An attentive one.

Janitor's Keyring

Risk doesn't bring a project to ash. Ignoring it does.

The Wisdom Within: Stone Soup

Once, in a village worn thin by crisis, the work had stopped. The people were tired. The doors stayed shut. Every household had something small to share, but no one spoke of it. Each person waited for someone else to fix what had gone quiet.

Then came three travelers. They carried no food. No answers. Simply a pot.

They stood in the square, cold, silent, and central, and set it down. They fetched water. They lit a fire. They placed three stones inside and began to stir.

"What are you doing?" asked a child.

"Making stone soup," they said. "It starts simple. But with a little help, it becomes something good."

The child stayed. So did the smoke. And soon, someone added salt. Then carrots. Then barley. Not because anyone was told to contribute, but because the stage was set: a fire, a pot, a reason to try.

One by one, the villagers stepped forward. A few onions. A bit of turnip. A slice of meat. What had felt like famine became food. What had felt like silence became rhythm. The soup fed everyone, not by magic, but because someone made space for others to bring what they had.

They ate together in the square, not just fed, but reconnected, neighbors again, not just survivors. And when the pot cooled and the fire dimmed, the stones remained. Not as an ingredient, but as a reminder of what can happen when someone sees what otherwise might have been ignored.

The project janitor doesn't arrive with a plan to feed the team. They arrive ready to rebuild the structure. They light the flame. They place the pot. And they wait, steady, watchful, for others to bring what they can.

No one is forced. No one is held to the fire. Once the frame exists, momentum begins.

Because even in projects, recovery doesn't begin with answers. It begins with arrangement, something simple, something steady, something solid enough to carry what comes next.

That's how risk becomes manageable: Not by expecting someone to bring everything, but by making it safe for everyone to bring something.
-- Traditional fable, as told by a Project Janitor

Adding to Your Toolbox

Contain the spill: Pause work that could amplify damage. Freeze updates based on outdated data. Create a visible boundary around the crisis to stop the spread.

Stabilize the system: Reopen the risk register. Reestablish communication using a single system of record. Ask what is still true, what has changed, and what needs to be made visible.

Restore structure: Set a central rhythm others can join. Rebuild with documentation, meeting cadence, and defined roles. Use visibility to anchor progress.

Remove what no longer applies: Identify duplicate reports, abandoned tools, and legacy plans. Clear what adds confusion instead of clarity.

Name every risk: Surface formal and informal risks. Sort them by impact, likelihood, ownership, and action. Give every risk a category and a place.

Track and assign ownership: Ensure every known risk has a clear owner. Replace vague tracking with shared systems that reflect actual movement.

Spot small wins: Look for evidence of recovery. A resolved blocker. A finished sprint. A clear answer. These are the first signs of regained trust.

Keep the soup boiling: Like in the fable, maintain steady rhythm. Do not demand contribution. Provide a frame. Progress comes when the team feels safe enough to join.

Chapter 8
The Janitor's Crew: Building Trust to Lead Your Team Forward

Executive Summary

Trust doesn't disappear with a bang. It erodes quietly, in the space between what was promised and what was delivered. By the time a project janitor is called, the shouting has already stopped. What's left is silent resignation. Meetings without momentum. Updates without ownership. Teams going through the motions. This chapter explores how to read that silence, how to recognize when belief in the project, or the culture, has left the room, and what it takes to rebuild it.

Trust doesn't reappear with a bang either. You won't fix trust with a better plan. You'll fix it by being stable, by noticing what others dismiss, and by resisting the urge to prove yourself too soon. This chapter focuses on the quiet work of rebuilding credibility. Not through speeches or structure, but through presence, pattern, and patience. We'll walk the rows. We'll listen for what's missing. And we'll revisit a time when the greatest risk wasn't the problem itself, but the team's decision to stop believing in solutions.

Trust, once lost, slowly ruins a project. And restoring it quietly and consistently is the project janitor's job.

The Mess at Hand

Mistrust doesn't always begin with betrayal. It begins with someone crying wolf. But this story is not about a wolf. Sometimes it starts with a crow. Or many. A peck here, a seed gone there. The boy saw them first, black shapes flitting through the corn. He shouted. Once, twice, louder each day. But the villagers were tired. They came the first few times, ran even, only to find stalks swaying in the breeze, no issues in the field. But today they came. The boy's voice grew hoarse. The corn grew thin. Yet the village stopped listening. Not out of spite, but exhaustion. That's how trust breaks. Not all at once. Not with one errant word. But with a quiet corrosion that settles in. And once it's gone, bringing it back is a project itself. Lost trust. That's why leadership calls for a project janitor.

The trouble is, by the time you arrive, the shouting has already stopped. You're not the one who cried crow. You're not the villagers. You're the one sent in when the corn is half-picked, the scarecrow leans, and no one bothers to look up anymore. The team may smile, nod, even say they're glad you're here. But the truth hangs quieter, worn into the way updates are filtered, questions softened, and meetings end without clarity. This is the field you've inherited. And no one is waiting for *your* voice.

Start by watching. How they enter the room. How they leave. Where the pauses fall, and who dares to fill them. Trust leaves traces when it departs. A hesitation before volunteering. A smile that doesn't reach the eyes. Tasks completed without conviction. Updates stripped to surface. No one says it aloud, but the crows hover over the field now, circling low, not landing. The team has gone quiet. Not because they're calm. Because they've stopped believing the sound was ever a signal at all. Your job isn't to interrupt. It's to understand what was lost, and why they stopped listening.

How does a project janitor begin to see the loss of trust and understand it? By noticing what others dismiss. A project janitor reads the room the way a botanist reads soil, testing for what's missing, not just what's visible. They don't chase symptoms. They trace patterns. A missed update isn't just a delay, it's a signal. It's a rustle in the trees. A short reply isn't just brevity, it's retreat. It's a shadow over the field. When trust is fractured, everything gets quieter, thinner, safer. You understand by resisting the urge to fix too soon. You walk the rows. You watch the crows. You listen. And you wait for the team to notice that someone's still there.

Notice the absences. The edits. The meetings where nothing feels wrong, but nothing moves forward. A project janitor doesn't need someone to say "we don't trust each other." They hear it in the flattening of tone, see it in the lack of follow-up, feel it in the way ideas are offered without eye contact. The loss of trust doesn't announce itself. It accumulates, like dust in corners no one admits to seeing. And the project janitor begins by seeing that dust for what it is: residue from something once shared, now withdrawn.

Everyone knows what happened. Marketing sold the contract with promises bigger than a plentiful field of corn. They handed the project to the PMO knowing much of the legalese wasn't likely deliverable in the pitched timeline. The trust didn't vanish in a single meeting; it eroded as teams worked late to meet dates they never believed in, while leadership clapped from the bleachers. It started with a mound. Now it's your mound. You've been handed the ball, but you don't start hurling. Not yet. That's the mistake. Rushing to fix trust is like repainting without priming. The shell won't hold. You show up without fanfare. Let the updates dry while you ask the questions no one's framed quite right. Let the silence stretch a little longer than they expect, just enough to prove you're not filling space. You're clearing it. Not everything broken needs a response. Some things need presence. Then, when it matters, pitch.

The Cleaning Strategy

OK. Let's swap the ball for the broom. Sweeping up starts with acknowledging the damage. The project janitor walks in with awareness. Trust has been lost. That's the baseline: the quiet, cumulative erosion of belief. You don't name names. You don't dissect the past. You read the room, the calendar, the tired lines on the team's faces. Progress begins when you accept that it's not your job to fix everything with a flourish. Your job is to be steady. Dependable without demanding attention. You're not there to earn praise. You're there to reestablish rhythm. Not to prove yourself, but to prepare the field so belief has somewhere to grow. Quietly. Gradually. In a way the team can absorb, not resist.

Trust starts small. Say what you will do. Then do it. Nothing fancy. No crying crow. Stay consistent. Promise the doable. Deliver. Repeat. That's the method. But when the ground is scorched from years of overcommitment, even that can feel ambitious. The team isn't waiting for a savior. They're watching for patterns. So don't start with big picture thinking. Start with reality. What's working. What's not. What's possible by Friday. Trim expectation until the shape is clean and clear. Then meet it. Again. And again. Let small truths stack. Let them stand on their own. Over time, they become something sturdier than hope. They become belief. Earned. Not demanded.

Take care not to overcorrect. When timelines collapse and teams wear thin, the instinct is to try to fix everything at once. But that kind of pressure only adds to the mess. The moment the team senses that you're chasing a fix-all fantasy, trust erodes further. Teams don't need a hero with a new plan. They need a safe space to speak, and someone secure enough to hear them. So you start by listening. What's been tried. What still works. What failed, and why. The project janitor doesn't chase reinvention. They look for what's salvageable and rebuild from there. Change must arrive in step with trust, not ahead of it. And trust doesn't return in a single meeting. It returns slowly when someone speaks up and isn't punished for it. When a risk is identified and the room leans in to help. When people stop bracing for disappointment and start looking ahead. That's when you know the cleanup is real. Trust is real. Still, if you push too soon, you'll lose it all again. Some lessons are best learned gently. Others leave a mark. We've seen what happens when trust is rushed. You'll see it too.

Scrub Away the Chaos

Scrubbing starts by paying attention to what the team does when they're not being prompted: who speaks up, who stalls, who silently reroutes the work. After trust breaks, the signs don't show up in dashboards, they show up in hesitation. The client skips calls. The vendor is late. Again. Work slows without explanation. Approvals drag because no one wants to be accountable. Status meetings get quieter, tighter. People stop saying "we" and start talking about "they." These aren't just bad habits. They're the residue of broken trust. If you try to push past them with a new process or a better plan, you'll miss the cleanup entirely. You're not fixing misalignment. You're treating something deeper, like the fear of naming broken priorities or calling out a risk no one wants to own.

So you start small. Not by reshaping the process, but by calling attention to what no longer lines up. You ask what's still valid and point to what clearly isn't. You surface what the team already sees: priorities slipped, roles blurred, and the system of record at odds with the real state of work. Then you say what others have been avoiding. This task is blocked. That one is idle. This milestone won't be met. Not to rattle the villagers, but to reopen the space for shared accountability. Recovery only begins when people believe you mean what you say. Bring confidence backed by preparation. Show your work. Explain your choices. Invite questions before conclusions. Bit by bit, the team starts to re-engage, even if you need to raise your voice, slightly, because you're not bluffing.

Still, even when you do everything right, when you listen first, speak plainly, and rebuild slowly, the ground can shift faster than the trust can hold. We thought we were steady. We saw the problem, mapped a clean fix, and assumed the team would carry it forward. On paper, the solution made perfect sense. But we missed what mattered most: they weren't ready. Not yet. The damage wasn't done to the plan. It was done to the belief behind it. And when you move too soon, even the right answer can land wrong. The project janitor doesn't just offer direction. They offer steadiness when the team has forgotten how to follow. They rebuild belief, not in themselves, but in the possibility of resuming progress. And they do it while standing in the wreckage left by someone else's vision.

Lessons from the Janitor's Closet

The French came first. Grand plans. Elegant sketches. Bold declarations about what would be built and how fast. They didn't just promise a canal, they promised to carve a shortcut through the continents. They pitched it like a marvel. But it failed. Spectacularly. The work was rushed. The terrain underestimated. The deaths from disease uncounted. What was left behind wasn't just a failed project but a broken belief in the project itself. By the time the Americans arrived, the idea of the Panama Canal had become a modern-day ruin. A cautionary tale. Even the workers, those who hadn't died, had given up entirely. The dirt was cursed, they said. The land didn't want to become a waterway.

But then came Stevens. Not a showman. A project janitor. An engineer who walked the site before updating a single plan. As a project janitor does, he started by stabilizing. Building trust. He set up housing. Supply lines. Sanitation. He saw that no amount of engineering would matter if the people doing the work didn't believe it could be done. His first act wasn't to dig, but to restore order. His second was to bring in Goethals, a builder with the same mindset: steady, sober, methodical. No big speeches. Just small wins. Day after day.

Together, they moved more than just dirt. They moved minds. They rebuilt belief. Quietly. Systematically. By fixing what was broken off the paper, so what was on the paper had a chance. In the end, the canal wasn't just a triumph of engineering. It was a triumph of patience. Of presence. Of trust, built slowly, like the canal, one prepared decision at a time.

That's the work. That's the project janitor's role. You don't just replace the plan. You restore trust. And the ground it's meant to stand on.

Spills and Cleanups

The danger of lost trust isn't just resistance, it's resignation. The team says they're on board, but inside, they've already stepped back. Cameras stay on. Passion stays off. You think you've earned alignment, but what you're hearing is avoidance. The project janitor arrives with steadiness but must take care not to mistake quiet for consent. A plan gets approved. Timelines are accepted. Roles confirmed. And still, the room feels thinner. Meetings run smooth. Risks appear minimal. Agreement comes easy. Then nothing moves. That's not trust returning. That's retreat, dressed as cooperation.

Sometimes the cleanup looks good. Too good. The board is organized. The meetings run on time. Roles are clarified, tools refreshed, dashboards green. But underneath the polish, nothing's connected. The energy isn't shared, it's scattered. The vendor spit shines a stale old deck, and the client remains silent throughout the update. The project janitor introduced structure before the team was ready to care. Ritual replaced relationship. Tasks moved because the process said so, not because the outcome mattered. Progress became performance. Everyone's doing their part, but not in the same direction. That's not traction. That's quiet compliance wrapped in calendar cadence. And when the results don't come, it won't be the process they question. It will be you. Trust. That must come first.

To be trusted is a greater compliment than to be loved.
--George MacDonald

Adding the Polish

How do you know you're trusted? It starts slowly. People hand you what they're afraid to carry alone. The real doubts. The things that could fail. The late-night email they almost didn't send. You're trusted when you're invited into the room before the decision is made, not just called to clean it up afterward. When someone shares a concern that could make them look bad, and they share it anyway. When they stop filtering. When the project's unvarnished truth finds its way to you without fanfare, because they believe you'll hold it steady. That's trust. Not blind agreement. Not visible harmony. Trust is when someone lets you see what they could have hidden, but didn't. The key is, they're not afraid you'll turn it against them. Don't.

You know you're trusted when people start bringing you the unfinished version. The half-thought. The early draft. When they don't wait for a polished answer because they are certain you'll help shape the right one. Without pointing a finger. You're trusted when someone flags a risk before it fully forms, not after it explodes. When a developer loops you in without being told. When the vendor pauses mid-update and asks, "Should we be looking at this differently?" These aren't grand gestures. They're quiet signals. Trust doesn't always come with a handshake. Sometimes it's just a CC line that wasn't there last week. Sometimes it's the moment you're asked to listen, not to fix, not to lead, but just to be present. Trust is truth.

The surest sign that trust has returned is when others start to work the way you do. Not by copying your methods, but by mirroring your intent. They say what they're going to do, then they do it. Quietly. Reliably. Not for credit, but because the team has become something worth honoring. You see initiative without fear, correction without blame, follow-through without prompting. The rhythm you brought becomes the rhythm they keep. That's what happened at the canal. Leadership adjusted, and the real transformation flowed downstream. Trust returned when presence became practice, when calm decisions, made one after another, began to echo through the ranks. That's the polish. Not the shine on the surface, but the strength beneath it. Earned. Repeated. Trusted.

Janitor's Keyring

Trust isn't declared. It's observed. It's offered to you in pieces, not all at once, and only when the stakeholders are ready. Don't rush it. Don't demand it. Watch what team members bring you when they think no one's looking. That's the truth of the work. And when trust begins to return, protect it. Hold it steady. Let it shine.

The Wisdom Within: The Boy Who Cried Crow

Once, there was a boy asked to watch a field. It wasn't much, just rows of young corn, a patch of fence, and a post with a tattered hat nailed on top. His job was simple: keep the crows away.

The first day, he saw them early. Black shapes against the sun, settling along the edge like shadows testing the line. They didn't touch the field. He shouted anyway. He tested the trust. He ran to the village and cried, "The crows are coming! The crows are coming!" And they came. Not the crows, the villagers. Pitchforks in hand. Dust rising behind them.

But the field was fine. The wind had stirred the stalks. Maybe a feather. Maybe not.

The next time, it was clearer. A real bird. Two. Still, no crows touched the field, but again he tested the trust. He shouted. And the villagers ran to the field. Again, the crows were nowhere in sight.

After a while, the villagers stopped running. The boy kept shouting, but no one came. The trust was gone. They had other fields. Other fears. And the corn still stood.

So when the crows came in silence, no one knew. Not at first. They didn't swarm. They didn't descend like stories warned. They picked one seed, one leaf, one morning at a time. By harvest, half the yield was missing. Not because of a single storm, but because no one believed the warning when it finally mattered.

Years later, another boy stood in that field. Same post. Same hat. But he didn't shout. He built a scarecrow and set it on the fence, under the hat. He walked the rows every morning. He watched the tree line, not the village. The crows came but often didn't stay. He held the field.

When the crows were too many to handle alone, the boy cried out to the villagers. They always came to assist.

He didn't demand trust. He earned it. Quietly, while no one was looking.

That's the project janitor's story. Not the one who cries, but the one who stays.

-- Based on Aesop's "The Boy Who Cried Wolf," retold here as the version of the story that I told my own children. Crows and corn, not wolves and sheep.

Adding to Your Toolbox

Acknowledge the loss: Begin by recognizing that trust has eroded. Do not assign blame or rush to fix it. Observe the team's behaviors and listen for what is no longer being said.

Read the room: Watch how people enter and exit meetings. Notice the tone, the edits, the hesitation. Understand trust not by what is spoken, but by what is withheld.

Be steady and visible: Resist the urge to perform. Show up with calm presence and dependable rhythm. Say what you will do, and do it, again and again.

Trim expectations: Start small. Identify what is possible now, this week, this sprint. Deliver on it. Let small promises build into quiet credibility.

Avoid pressure tactics: Do not chase the illusion of a single fix. Invite the team to speak. Rebuild shared space before you restructure the process.

Surface misalignment: Call out what no longer lines up. Point to idled tasks, blocked items, and stale assumptions. Say what others have avoided, clearly and respectfully.

Earn confidence, do not demand it: Explain your decisions. Show your work. Invite questions. Rebuild the belief that truth can be spoken and acted upon.

Align change with readiness: Implement change only when the team is ready to accept it. Do not outpace trust. Reassure through preparation, not pressure.

Reinforce trust with consistency: Look for small wins and steady signs of re-engagement. A question asked. A risk flagged. A quiet contribution offered without fear.

Mirror the rhythm you want to see: Model honesty, patience, and follow-through. When others begin to work that way too, trust has begun to return.

Chapter 9
Mopping Up Missed Minutes: Managing Time and Deadlines

Executive Summary

Projects rarely collapse in a moment. Time doesn't fail loudly - it slips, task by task, hour by hour, while calendars stay full and scope remains untouched. This chapter explores how project janitors recognize, recover, and prevent the erosion of time midstream. Instead of pushing teams to move faster, they walk the timeline backward to restore what time flows through: the critical path, dependencies, sequences. Commitments. From missed milestones and stalled deployments to punch lists buried beneath headlines, they don't chase the clock. They clear the path. And when they do, everything moves again, in time.

The Mess at Hand

The mess of missed minutes never starts with the clock. It starts with a breathless pause. The moment you look at the second hand and it takes a millennium to advance. The sense that something should have happened by now but hasn't. Meetings have multiplied, but movement has stalled. You arrive to find progress frozen mid-stride. Tasks half-picked. Milestones half-met. People staring at each other across a canyon of slipped minutes. The calendar is full, but the work queue isn't moving. And somewhere, beneath the surface of it all, time is leaking. Not loudly. Not in Westminster chimes. More like a quiet, slow drip behind a wall. Warping the frame. Softening the floor. Rotting the foundation long before anyone smells the mold.

Most teams don't notice at first. Not because they're careless, but because they're busy. They meet. They reply. They schedule. They send reminders. The drip becomes the backdrop. Delays renamed as dependencies. Waiting is rebranded as coordination. And soon, no one can say when the work was last ahead of the clock. Schedules keep getting kicked to the right. The rhythm of the project becomes the rhythm of delay, late starts, half-done handoffs, status updates that report the passage of time instead of progress through it. It's not chaos, really. It's a slow settling. Like dust on a windowsill that few notice.

The project janitor sees it, though. Not by intuition alone, but by following the critical path. Through the discipline of walking the work breakdown or backlog, line by line, and asking: What came before this? What was supposed to precede it? Who owns the gate? They track not just what's late, but what's quietly stalled. Tasks that should be complete but sit unconfirmed. Predecessors marked done while their outputs lie untouched. Tickets lost in queues. They notice when status reports celebrate motion over completion. Burning down hours is not enough when the remaining scope stands still. When effort is spent, yet no artifacts move forward. To the project janitor, time loss isn't a mystery. It's a trail of skipped steps and unchecked boxes. Recapturing time begins not with urgency, but with order.

The Cleaning Strategy

Project janitors don't race the clock. They stabilize it. Their first move isn't to push the team to move faster, it's to check their rhythm. What's missing? What's out of sync? What's been marked complete that never moved? They return to the backlog again and again for clarity. If the schedule has slipped, they walk it until the reason behind the slip becomes visible. If the structure feels brittle, they press gently at the joints to find where it gives. And if no one can explain why the team is behind, they follow the task flow until they find where progress fell through the floor. Because managing time isn't about squeezing the day but sealing the leak.

Some projects run late because of poor estimates. Others fall behind because someone promised speed before they understood the sequence. It's easy to believe that progress is just a matter of trying harder, adding people, double-booking meetings, lighting a fire. But acceleration without alignment is how messes multiply. You can't outrun disarray. And throwing bodies at it? You can't always crash the project. More people may not be the solution. After all, only so many boots can surround the slab. The faster you move with no control, the faster things flood. The project janitor has seen what happens when ambition acts without architecture. They don't try to conjure motion. They slow the spin just enough to label it.

Cleaning up missed minutes doesn't always begin with the next sprint. It begins with a checklist. The project janitor rebuilds the timeline, not through a rose-colored Gantt chart, but from the real sequence of what happened, what's blocked, and what still holds weight. They redraw the critical path and every other with slack by walking them, not wishing with guestimates. Milestones are revalidated. Task owners re-engaged. Soft commitments become visible promises. And every dependency is tested, one by one, like pressure-checking a pipe. If the delay stems from a security concern, it's logged. If the stall lives in stakeholder indecision, it's escalated. If the path no longer leads anywhere real, it's routed or eliminated. Because cleaning time isn't about going faster but restoring flow.

This approach works because time loss in a project is about the structure that surrounds it. Most teams try to reclaim schedule by increasing velocity, pushing harder, adding bodies, working late. But if the underlying sequence is misaligned, those extra hours don't move the work forward. They just stir the chaos. The project janitor reclaims time by restoring the structure that time flows through. When dependencies are clarified, blockers named, and effort tied to visible outcomes, time doesn't need to be created, it's revealed. The delay wasn't always in the lack of doing. It was in the waiting, the confusion, the half-owned handoffs. This is why rebuilding the timeline; walking the work breakdown or backlog; and resetting the gatekeepers isn't bureaucracy. It's recovery. Because once structure returns, progress can flow. And when it doesn't? Let's find out.

Scrub Away the Chaos

Scrubbing the schedule never starts with a new, boilerplate template. It starts with the mess as it is. The project janitor doesn't panic at the sight of a red-lined project plan, or a milestone pushed six times. They dissect the work breakdown or product backlog. They look at the old estimates, ready to clean up a crime scene. Why did the original project leader set this date? Based on what? What gate was skipped, and who waved it through? Why are the stories still unclear? What happened during grooming? The project janitor doesn't ask for a new plan. They build the one that should have been followed all along by tracking what was missed and why it mattered. And in the middle of that quiet, tedious work, they find the pattern: the meetings where decisions slipped. The tickets no one escalated. The week the network circuit team waited for someone to open a locked door, then left when no one did. That's when cleanup becomes narrative. And narrative, told honestly, becomes time reclaimed.

So they started with the missed site. The one where the circuit team had shown up on schedule, found the server room locked, and left without logging a delay. No one had rescheduled. No one had escalated. It just sat. Days passed. Then weeks. The milestone stayed red, but the comment thread said nothing. The project janitor pulled the access logs. Called facilities. Found the person who had the key, and the person who thought someone else had followed up. They logged the miss and rewrote the task as what it had become, not a circuit activation, but a recovery. That single site became the pattern. Other visits had gone just as silent. Doors locked. Teams waiting. Time slipping. The project janitor started tagging each of them, one by one. Not for blame. For sequencing. Because if you don't identify where time was lost, you can't chart a path to get it back.

Let's go big. It wasn't just site work where time slipped. Boston's Big Dig, launched in 1991 and planned for completion by 1998, lost years one missed decision at a time. Materials delayed. Oversight thinned. Contractors left to self-manage while design flaws went unflagged, and approvals fell weeks behind the work. By the time accountability showed up, the calendar was a graveyard of unkept promises. But even that project, bloated and politicized, eventually found its project janitors. Engineers who reopened the task sequences. Oversight teams who tracked the lag back to its source: missing specs, flawed contracts, doors that had been closed for too long. They didn't rescue the original schedule. That was gone. Lost somewhere in the harbor. But they reclaimed what was left of the timeline by making the work honest again. No illusions. No shortcuts. Just structural discipline where ambition had once run wild.

And under it all, the Ted Williams Tunnel kept leaking. Not just water, but time. Concrete sections misaligned. Seals that should have held under pressure gave way. Inspections flagged flaws, but paperwork floated downstream while crews stood idle uptown. It was supposed to be open by 1995. It did open, barely. Locals were cautious because the list of incomplete items read like an indictment: ventilation tests skipped, ceiling panels rushed, quality logs missing entire sections. It took another decade, and the weight of tragedy, before anyone took the final punch list seriously. Only then did the project janitors return. Not with new blueprints, but with rework orders, hardhats, and the quiet resolve to finish what had been oversold and mistimed. They didn't fix history. But they made the structure safe. And in the end, that mattered far more than finishing fast.

Lessons from the Janitor's Closet

Some project timeline meltdowns begin with good intentions and the wrong sequence. Someone sees a task that looks simple. They act. Not out of laziness, but impatience. Not out of defiance, but eagerness to help, to impress, to move. The problem isn't the motion but what gets set in motion. A process is started without understanding how to stop it. Work begins before anyone has checked the gates, confirmed the steps, tested the flow. And at first, it looks like progress. Tasks stir. Resources churn. Then the backlog clogs, the dependencies collapse, and what started as initiative becomes a flood. You don't get time back by reacting faster. You get it back by restoring stability. That's what the project janitor brings. Not magic. Not speed. Instead, they bring presence, process, and the quiet discipline to shut down what was never ready to run.

There was once an apprentice who was left alone with tools they didn't fully understand. The cleanup was supposed to be simple, routine even. But they wanted to impress. To move fast. To show they could lead. So they set things in motion before learning how things operate. At first, everything moved. Water poured, systems spun up, work appeared to flow. But without stability, the effort grew wild. The room didn't get cleaner. It flooded. The very tools meant to help had been unleashed without order. And when the mess finally overwhelmed them, it wasn't noise or speed that saved the day. It was the return of someone who understood flow, who had the presence to stop what never should have started, and the patience to mop what ambition had drowned.

It's easy to forget that the chaos wasn't sabotage. It was urgency, acted out too early, without sequence, without understanding. The tools did exactly what they were told. They didn't improvise. They followed orders, over and over, until the floor vanished under a flood of effort. That's the part we often miss. The mess, the wasted time, wasn't made by inaction. It was made from motion without progress. And the one who started it? Not evil. Just eager. Just untrained. It took someone else to stop it. Someone who knew the order, the limits, the weight of the work. Someone who didn't need spells. Just a mop, a bucket, and the wherewithal to drain what ambition had overrun. That's the story of the project that arrived late. That's the story of the Sorcerer's Apprentice.

The story matters because it still happens, every day. Not in castles, but in conference rooms. Not with spells, but with systems launched before they're ready. Timelines that were once clear and sequenced begin to slip. What should have progressed according to plan, whether through a critical path or a program increment, starts to slip. Time disappears not because no one is working, but because hours are burned without burning scope. Tasks are marked active, but nothing moves forward. And no one knows how to stop it. That's why every project needs someone who has seen this before. Someone who can walk the timeline backward so a workable plan can move forward. Someone who knows when to pause, when to escalate, when to clean. Because once time is lost, all that matters next is to take ownership of how it was spent.

Spills and Cleanups

Time doesn't fail all at once. It drains out slowly, as time will, through forgotten follow-ups, slipped handoffs, and plans that were never confirmed out loud. By the time anyone notices, the calendar looks full, but the work hasn't moved. The hours are gone. The scope remains.

The telephony project was supposed to modernize the entire phone system, statewide, site by site. A full migration from copper lines to voice over IP, VOIP. But it stalled early. Meetings stacked up, yet site work lagged. Circuit teams showed up to locked doors. No one answered their calls. No one rescheduled. No one followed up. The original project leader kept pushing the schedule forward but never monitored the critical path. By the time the project janitor stepped in, fourteen counties still had no dial tone. Tasks were marked complete. Dependencies went unresolved. Over six weeks, the project janitor tracked the delay to its source: access, approvals, accountability. They rewrote the rollout sequence based on what was real, not what was once promised. Phones started ringing again. Not through speed, but through ownership.

Some lessons outlast the mess. In project work, we learn them through missed milestones, delayed rollouts, and the long road back from good intentions. But time, when used well, leaves a different mark. It doesn't disappear. It holds the door open just long enough for someone willing to clear the path.

Time stays long enough for those who use it.
-- Leonardo da Vinci

Adding the Polish

How do you know project timing is back on track? You know when the calendar stops lying. When dates mean something again. When meetings don't drag but deliver. You hear it in the updates: shorter, clearer, tighter. No one has to fake confidence or guess where things stand. The scope starts shrinking instead of shifting. Handoffs happen without drama. Delays don't vanish, but they surface early; they're tagged, owned, and addressed. It's not speed that tells you timing is right, it's alignment. The plan matches the progress. Burn-downs burn scope, not just hours. And the team, once reactive, starts looking ahead again.

It doesn't always feel like a victory. Sometimes, getting back on track means letting go of what was promised. Reworking what was rushed. Telling the truth about what can still be done, and by when. But that's the polish. Not the spin, not the speed, not the illusion of progress shining on a slide, but the clarity that comes after a real cleanup. When the work aligns with the clock again, even imperfect progress can move with confidence. And that's what you leave behind when the timing is right: not just a project on schedule, but a team that can trust the calendar again.

Back to the dial tone debacle, calls were routing within a few weeks of the project janitor's arrival. Not just in the capital, but in every outlying site. The circuit teams stopped showing up to locked doors. The tickets stopped aging in silence. Status reports came in shorter because there was less to explain. Not everything was perfect. Some fixes took longer than expected, and the original schedule never fully recovered. But the pace gained momentum. The missed minutes were no longer multiplying. They were accounted for. That's what the project janitor left behind. A dial tone. A satisfied client. Nothing unfinished.

Janitor's Keyring

Too bad that cleaning the clock can't bring back lost time. So instead, clean the path. Missed minutes don't return just because you rush. Burned hours don't come back with pressure. That's why project janitors don't try to recover time by moving faster. They recover time by restoring what flows through it: the critical path, dependencies, sequences. Features, stories, commitments. Do the work.

The Wisdom Within: The Apprentice Who Flooded the Floor

There was once someone left in charge before they were ready. They had seen the process. Watched the master work the system - valves opened in order, buckets filled and emptied with care. But watching isn't knowing. And when the master stepped away, the apprentice saw the mess, the tools, and the chance to prove they could handle it.

So they acted.

They reached for the shortcut trying to save time. They skipped the checklist. Set the automation running without knowing how to shut it off. And for a moment, it looked like progress. The brooms swept. The water flowed. The room sparkled with motion. But the apprentice hadn't learned the rollback. They didn't understand the gates. What began as a shortcut became a system out of control. And a cleanup that lost time.

The water rose. The brooms multiplied. Effort filled the space, but none of it was coordinated. There was no sequence. No structure. Only unstable activity, spinning into chaos.

And by the time the master returned, the floor was underwater.

That kind of mess doesn't only happen in stories. It happens in real projects. We saw it when a tunnel was rushed to ribbon-cutting while the punch list was still a secret. When ceiling panels were fast-tracked and structural reviews postponed. When time slipped quietly out the side door while the headlines rolled in.

It took another team to make it right. They didn't show up with magic. They showed up with mops, buckets, and rework orders. They didn't recover the lost time. They restored what flows through it.

That's the difference.

Project janitors don't chase the clock.

They clear the path.

And everything moves again, in time.

-- J. W. von Goethe, as told by a Project Janitor

Adding to Your Toolbox

Recognize the leak: Time loss starts as hesitation. When updates grow vague, milestones repeat, or meetings stall without progress, look closer. These are signs that the project is slipping, even if the calendar looks full.

Walk the timeline backward: Before adding urgency, trace the path. Start at the stalled task and work in reverse to identify what came before it, what was skipped, and where ownership lapsed.

Validate the sequence: Redraw the critical path based on what actually happened. Check each dependency for relevance, alignment, and risk. Eliminate what no longer serves the project.

Look for soft commitments: Find tasks marked complete that never moved forward. Confirm ownership. Turn informal approvals and assumptions into visible, accountable actions.

Reclaim task ownership: Meet with task owners to restate expectations. Address blockers. Document handoffs. Realign assignments with what each role can realistically deliver.

Clean up the backlog: Examine every item for clarity, purpose, and sequence. Retire outdated stories. Rewrite vague tasks. Turn unresolved dependencies into visible blockers.

Reschedule with reality: Shift away from legacy timelines. Build a new schedule based on facts, not feelings. Adjust velocity to reflect what the team can sustainably complete.

Avoid false urgency: Resist the pressure to add people or rush deliverables. Acceleration without alignment makes the mess worse. Fix the structure first.

Restore rhythm: Replace scattered effort with intentional movement. Let each cleaned task make room for the next. Celebrate progress that frees flow, not speed alone.

Confirm that alignment has returned: You'll know it's working when tasks move again without drama, calendars match real progress, and the team begins to look ahead with confidence.

Chapter 10
Holding the Janitor's Keys: Navigating Accountability and Authority

Executive Summary

This chapter confronts one of the most enduring project realities: you are held accountable for outcomes without being granted the authority to achieve them. In matrixed environments, authority often lives elsewhere, locked in boardrooms, buried in outdated plans, or scattered across silos, while the cleanup falls squarely to you.

The project janitor must recognize that this misalignment is not an exception but the system itself. Success comes not from demanding control, but from creating clarity, building rhythm, and reinforcing boundaries before the structure collapses. You don't wait for permission to lead. You lead by holding the line, documenting decisions, and steadying the frame until others follow your pace. The role isn't about being in charge but about making the work hold.

The Mess at Hand

In a matrix organization, they toss you the keys, but not the one named Master. Just enough to open the supply closet, maybe the back stairwell. But not the server room. Not the boardroom. Not the drawer where the old decisions are locked away. Still, the cleanup falls to you. The milestone dates stay live, impossible or not, and your clock is already ticking. You're expected to scrub the sludge from a schedule you didn't create, polish deliverables you didn't design, and explain delays rooted in decisions you never made. You carry the weight, but not the authority.

PLAYBOOK FOR PROJECT JANITORS

The problems are plain to see: resources misaligned, approvals missing, priorities shuffled without notice. But you alone can't authorize the fix. The doors that control flow remain locked. Authority lives elsewhere. But the accountability? That lives with you. Every day. Written on your face. Pressed into your hands.

So you start adjusting. You push for a decision while the chain of command tables the motion. You move forward without answers because stopping isn't an option. You clear one blocker, then another, never sure where the mess began or where it ends. When access is denied, you find another way in. When the decision-maker disappears, you write the update yourself. You reroute around locked doors and burned time, not because it's efficient, but because it's the only way forward. At first, you expect the pattern to raise concern. You think someone above will spot the delays, the lack of access, the misalignment, and step in. But no one does. So you stop waiting. You do the work anyway. Because if you don't, it won't get done.

You stop chasing the perfect fix and start focusing on forward motion. Any motion. You learn which shortcuts still lead somewhere and which only loop back. You stop waiting for access and start building trust, not with a speech, but with presence. With follow-through. With meeting notes that catch what others miss, and a tone that calms the room. Progress doesn't come from title or command. It comes from traction. One steady step at a time, even when the floor keeps shifting beneath you. But how far can you walk without the authority to draw the line? The fisherman kept walking too.

The mess began as a wish without a boundary. The fisherman's wife held the desire. The fish held the power. But the fisherman carried the request, and the consequences. He had no authority to grant or deny, only to deliver. The wife never spoke to the fish. The fish never questioned the wish. And the fisherman, accountable for what followed, walked the same path each time, caught between command and compliance. The demands kept growing. The stakes kept rising. No one named the goal. No one set a boundary. The outcome wasn't chaos per se. It was compliance, silent escalation disguised as progress. Sound familiar? Each new milestone arrived faster than the last, each one stacked on a foundation never built to hold them. And through it all, the fisherman kept walking, carrying the request but never the authority behind it. That's the shape of the mess. Not a storm. A tide.

The Cleaning Strategy

Some messes are bright, beaming in your face. Others are subtle, hiding shadowlike against a project's back wall. When accountability and authority drift apart, the mess creeps in as agreement. The plan is accepted. The milestones make sense. The status reports show green. But beneath the surface, authority is misaligned. The person making the decisions isn't the one carrying the risk. The one held accountable isn't allowed to steer. And no one is brave enough, or clear enough, to say it. So the work continues, shaped by expectation but not guided by ownership. The project moves, but not forward. It spins. It repeats. It grows heavier by the day, until someone finally asks: who is allowed to draw the line?

The fable of the fisherman doesn't offer a clean finish. It offers a warning. When no one owns the boundary, the tide decides where things stop. That's why the project janitor doesn't wait for collapse. You step in before the structure gives way. You look for approaching surf. Who is deciding? Who is delivering? You identify the gaps others ignore. Not loudly. Not politically. Plainly and early enough that the foundation can still be saved. Because the cleanup, in this kind of mess, isn't about undoing what has been wished for. It is about stopping the escalation before the project stalls, breaks trust, or gets quietly shut down.

The project janitor doesn't need full authority to stop the drift. Just clarity. You make the model visible. Who owns the outcome? Who approves the changes? Who carries the risk? If the answers do not line up, you clarify them. Not as a complaint, but as a condition. A truth the team has to work within or change. And if no one else draws the line, you mark it anyway. In a meeting recap. In the risk register. In the part of the plan where wishful thinking meets real constraints. Because once the boundaries are visible, the escalation has somewhere to stop. The line has been drawn.

Still, drawing the line is just the start. Holding it takes rhythm, presence, and structure. The project janitor doesn't carry authority by title. You can earn it, however, by showing up and staying consistent. You lead collaborative decision maker meetings between vendors and clients, not just to share updates, but to keep priorities from fluctuating. These are not status meetings. They are traction points. Anchors. A place where the work gets realigned, blockers are discussed, and decisions are documented before they disappear into memory. You run weekly syncs across delivery leads to prevent misunderstanding from compounding. You establish regular leadership calls, not to impress executives, but to keep the line visible at the top. You remind sponsors what was agreed to, where the risk sits, and what it means to cross the boundary. Point to the line. You do not escalate with emotion. You escalate with facts, timing, and traceability. The line does not hold itself. You hold it by referencing it, returning to it, and refusing to let it fade.

Strategy gives you shape. Discipline gives you grip. Once the line is visible, the real work begins. Holding it requires more than awareness. It takes consistent action, grounded routines, and the kind of follow-through that clears the fog, not just marks the boundary. This is how the project janitor turns alignment into traction, one step at a time, through structured, repeatable work.

Scrub Away the Chaos

OK. Lines are drawn. How do we scrub away the chaos? Start the holding pattern with meetings. Not just any meetings, but the right ones, with the right rhythm. A standing project lead sync keeps the delivery leads aligned. A bi-weekly or even weekly leadership checkpoint keeps the lines visible and the priorities intact. Each meeting and each line serves a purpose: prevent drift, expose blockers, and reinforce the plan that was agreed to. Do not let these meetings become status rituals. Keep them alive. Log decisions. Discuss risks. Trace every change back to impact. These touchpoints are where alignment either holds or unravels. Make them hold.

Once the meetings are in place, the real test is what survives between them. The project janitor does not assume decisions will be upheld just because they were spoken aloud. Document them. Time-stamp them. Get them into the system of record, your intake system. You name who agreed and what they agreed to. And then you follow up, not only as a reminder, but to ensure no one redirects the plan in the span between the meetings. You don't chase alignment, you document it. When someone tries to walk back a choice, you bring the recap. When a change request appears that contradicts what was approved, you point to the history. If a decision is real, it gets recorded. When it's recorded, it's respected.

Priorities rarely blow up. They tend to wander. One conversation at a time, they float, until the team is chasing ten things with half the clarity. The project janitor holds the line by returning to the original agreement. You remind sponsors what the scope includes, and what it doesn't. You track what was deferred or dropped to keep it from creeping back in through the side door. You ask questions when new work appears. Where did this come from? What are we trading to get it done? Because in every story, the wishes seem small at first. The wife asked. The fisherman delivered. The fish said yes. But no one marked the limit. And no one held the line. You don't resist change. You resist forgetting. Your job isn't to say yes to everything. It's to remember what was already said. We don't just do what we're told. We do what's right.

Project-based resistance is rarely shaped like a rebellion. Most of the time, it takes the form of silence. A team member nods in the meeting, then goes back to doing it the old way. A stakeholder smiles but withholds the information you asked for. Others say yes, then do whatever they want. The project janitor doesn't escalate every moment of friction. You observe. You follow up. You ask again, calmly, clearly, and in writing. You don't argue. You keep the teams steady by focusing on the work. And when poor patterns continue, you label them as risks. Register them. You are not here to force compliance. You are here to protect the structure long enough for it to work. That takes steadiness, not a louder voice. Bring quiet clarity every time balance is tested. With that kind of consistency, assumed authority becomes granted.

Lessons from the Janitor's Closet

Michelangelo didn't ask to lead. He was handed someone else's plan. A grand, overbuilt, half-finished monument to ambition. St. Peter's Basilica had already burned through architects, competing drafts, collapsing timelines, and the patience of the papacy. The foundation was under strain. The costs were spiraling. And the original designer, Bramante, was long gone. Yet the Church expected progress. The people expected glory. And the Pope expected results. This project was too big to fail, and far too visible to stall.

So, in stepped the Renaissance man, not as chief architect, but as a servant to the vision. He wasn't granted full authority. Still, he inherited full accountability. If the dome collapsed, so did his reputation. Maybe even more. Failure in Rome, under papal patronage, wasn't just professional ruin. It could mean disgrace, exile, or worse. But Michelangelo didn't toss out the original plan. He studied it. Clarified it. He removed what didn't support the load. He simplified the form. And piece by piece, he made it whole.

That's the project janitor's path. You assume the accountability and garner the authority. You rarely start clean. You inherit a blueprint already in motion. The plan is not blank, it's bloated. Half-finished decisions. Conflicting documents. Layered assumptions. No one wants to revisit the foundation. They want it finished. As the Renaissance janitor, your job is not to question the ambition. It's to reconcile the structure. You study the framing. You test the weight. You look for what can hold and what cannot. Because once a project is built on shaky assumptions, no amount of polish will keep it standing. You may not have signed off on the plan, but you are still the one expected to make it stand when the pressure builds.

Simplification isn't weakness. It's reinforcement. The project janitor doesn't reduce the magnitude of the mission. You trim the excess. You consolidate timelines that no longer match capacity. You collapse duplicate requirements. You remove deliverables no one is willing to own. Quietly, carefully, you reduce complexity until the structure can stand on its own. You're not shrinking the vision. You're making the system stable. Michelangelo didn't shrink the dome or change the objective. He reshaped the project so it could carry its own weight. That's your role too. You don't erase the vision. You make it possible.

Even in most projectized organizations, project leaders don't have full authority. So don't expect it. You will step in late, carry the weight, and navigate a system that still answers to someone else. Michelangelo didn't outrank his predecessors. He didn't gain control through title. He earned the right to lead by staying steady, by showing up, and by doing the work. You do the same. You don't shout to be heard. You speak with consistency, with structure, and with calm. Over time, the team starts looking to you, not for permission, but for alignment. You don't demand control. You create the conditions where trust transfers naturally. When project teams sense stability, they have no use for panic. And when that happens, they'll let you steer.

Michelangelo finished the dome. The largest of its kind in the world at the time, built not by command, but by conviction. He was not granted full authority when the work began. But history gave it to him anyway. His name endures not because he demanded control, but because the structure stood. Beautifully. The Basilica still towers over Rome today, solid, centered, and complete. That is the legacy of the project janitor's path. The quiet authority that settles in after the work holds. When the project is finished and the scaffolding comes down, the one who made sure it didn't fall is the reason it stands at all.

Spills and Cleanups

As we've learned, not every mess bursts onto the floor. Some spill slowly, soaking through progress before anyone notices the damage. When accountability and authority split apart, traction is lost first. Status reports still read green. Meetings sound agreeable. But the work starts dragging. Deliverables stall without explanation. Approvals hang in limbo. And the project janitor can feel it before anyone else admits it. You're burning effort but not moving forward. Not because the team isn't working, but because no one has the clarity or control to move the real impediments.

Misalignment doesn't arrive with a bang. It seeps in. Quietly. Until nothing is broken, but nothing works.

When that structure starts to slip, the temptation is to keep your head down and carry the load. To deliver without challenging. To say yes without pause. But that kind of compliance doesn't protect the project, it buries it. If you accept every task without surfacing the misalignment, drawing the line, you inherit the blame for a collapse you didn't cause. That's the trap. You become the face of failure, even if you were never given the means to succeed. The fisherman never questioned the wish. He walked the same path, over and over, until the weight of unchecked escalation brought everything down. The mess didn't come from disobedience. It came from silence.

The project janitor never waits for permission to label what's broken. You clarify the model. You document the roles. You mark where the work should stop and who has the right to move it forward. You log the risk when decisions stall. You note the moment when approvals lapse. You document the blockers. You close the gap before the project falls through it. And if no one else will question the scope creep, you will. Because when the history is written, the record will show you saw it. You named it. And you held the line.

Rank does not confer privilege or give power. It imposes responsibility.
-- Peter Drucker

Adding the Polish

Accountability without authority is not a flaw in the system. It *is* the system. And once you understand that you stop expecting the structure to change before you act. You learn to lead from the inside out. Not by reshaping roles, but by reshaping rhythm. By showing up. By documenting what was said, honoring what was agreed, and returning to it, until others do the same.

You're not there to fix the hierarchy. You're there to keep the project standing within it. And when you do that well, the structure starts to move your way. Not because you demanded it, but because your presence made space for it. You didn't need the Master key. You needed the clarity to see the locks, find the keyholders, and keep the steadiness to make the work move no matter what.

Janitor's Keyring

You won't always be given control. But you will be given the work. And that's enough when you know how to keep the structure steady when the roles around you blur.

The Wisdom Within: The Fisherman and His Wife

There was once a poor fisherman who lived with his wife in a small, rundown hut near the sea. Each day, he cast his line into the waves, as fishermen do. One morning, he caught a remarkable fish, golden and glimmering, who spoke.

"Please let me go," said the fish, "for I am no ordinary fish. I am an enchanted prince."

Moved by mercy, the fisherman tossed the fish back and returned home.

When he told his wife what happened, she was furious.

"Why didn't you ask for something in return?" she demanded. "Go back. Tell the fish we want a cottage instead of this filthy hut."

Reluctantly, the fisherman returned to the shore. The sea had grown slightly darker. Still, he called the fish, who appeared and granted the request.

They received the cottage, but the wife was not content for long. Soon she asked for a castle. Then to be queen. Then empress. Then pope. And each time, the fisherman walked to the sea, the tide rising, the water growing rougher and darker with each visit. And each time, the fish granted the wish. Without question, without protest.

Finally, the wife asked to be like God, to command the sun and moon. The fisherman, weary and broken, returned to the sea. The sky had turned black. The wind howled. He called the fish one last time and delivered the message.

The fish did not respond with a loud voice or in anger. It simply said, "Go home." And when the fisherman returned, the castle was gone. The wife, once a pope, once an empress, once a queen, was back in the filthy hut. They had nothing. No more wishes. No more answers. Just the beginning, all over again.

The lesson is not about greed. It's about escalation without structure. The fisherman never questioned the request. The fish never questioned the cost. The wife never questioned the limit. That's how misalignment becomes collapse: from absence of clarity, of boundaries, of ownership.

The project janitor's role is to notice when momentum has turned into unchecked drift. To question the next wish when no one else will. To remember what was already said and to make sure what's built can hold. Don't let the tide decide where things stop. Hold the line.

--Brothers Grimm, as told by a Project Janitor

Adding to Your Toolbox

Recognize the system: Understand that accountability without authority is not an exception. It is the norm in matrixed environments. Accept the structure without being constrained by it.

Walk the project's structure: Study the plan you inherited. Trace ownership, decision rights, and delivery responsibility. Identify where expectations are misaligned with control.

Mark the misalignment: Clarify who approves, who delivers, and who carries risk. If the answers do not match, document the gap. Say it early. Say it plainly.

Draw the line: Make the boundary visible. Where does the scope stop? What triggers escalation? What is non-negotiable? If no one else names the limit, you do.

Set up the anchors: Establish rhythm through standing syncs and checkpoints. Keep leadership aligned. Prevent drift by making the plan a living part of the calendar.

Document decisions: Record every agreement. Capture who said yes, what they said yes to, and when. When the wind shifts, return to the record. If it's not written, it didn't happen.

Prevent silent drift: Track scope that was deferred, dropped, or redirected. Stop it from creeping back in. If it reappears, ask what tradeoff is being made.

Surface quiet resistance: Watch for smiles with no follow-through. Label patterns. Log unkept promises as risks. Bring clarity, not confrontation.

Earn authority through rhythm: Lead with steadiness. Return to the plan. Respect the roles. The more consistent you are, the more others will follow your pace.

Simplify what must hold: Trim the excess. Collapse duplicate efforts. Clarify what matters. Reinforce the structure before pressure mounts.

Don't wait to be granted control: You don't need the Master key. You need clarity, rhythm, and the will to hold the structure when others let it drift.

Chapter 11
Unclogging the Drain: Staying Grounded While Monitoring Progress

Executive Summary

Chapter 11 confronts one of the most quietly dangerous blurs in project delivery: the illusion of steady progress without true oversight. It's not always chaos that derails a project. Sometimes it's simply small things unmonitored. When updates sound optimistic, dashboards stay green, and no one verifies the results, small divergences build beneath the surface until they harden into systemic failures.

This chapter explores the project janitor's role in grounding motion in truth. Monitoring is not micromanagement. It is the practice of seeing clearly. Project janitors read between updates, align baselines with behavior, and restore confidence through visibility. From undocumented omissions to misaligned assumptions, the early signs of erosion are subtle. That is why the project janitor stays focused.

Drawing lessons from the Hubble Space Telescope repair and a real-world Enterprise Resource Planning (ERP) recovery effort, the chapter shows how monitoring protects trust, schedule, and scope. It ends with a reminder: polish is not decoration; it is inspection. Monitoring does not just prevent failure. It confirms clarity. It confirms recovery.

The Mess at Hand

A project once shifted shape every time someone looked at it. Each update rewrote its purpose. Each new voice pulled it in a different direction. Team members claimed progress, but no one could explain what had really moved. The problem wasn't its inertia but its unmonitored motion. Ungrounded. Like the miller and his son, who first walked beside their donkey, then rode it, then carried it to please the crowd, the team lost their footing. They didn't stall; they quietly wandered off course. And by the time anyone noticed, the donkey was gone.

Some failures strike fast. This one takes shape slowly, hidden beneath the illusion of motion. Teams file updates. Metrics rise. The dashboard beams. But something feels off. Missing. Conversations grow thinner. Adjustments happen without formal revisions. A deadline pushes to the right, and no one recalibrates the sequence downstream. The surface shows progress, the trajectory looks on target, yet the structure starts to sway. It is not sabotage. It is erosion, quiet and cumulative, and rarely challenged until something slips.

In these moments, the project janitor doesn't rush to act. They watch. They walk the corridors, virtual or physical. Floor by floor. Not only to inspect, but to listen, to pace the rhythm of the team against the tempo of the plan. Monitoring is not micromanagement. It is alignment. It is the work of noticing when the grout no longer holds, when a once-straight hallway now veers, even slightly. The project janitor knows a project can move at full speed and still be heading in the wrong direction.

The danger isn't delay but the illusion that none exists. When false progress goes unchecked, stakeholders stay comfortable, vendors stay quiet, and teams stay tired. By the time someone raises a concern, the problem has compounded beneath layers of unchallenged assumptions. That is when the project janitor steps in to recalibrate, not to waive a finger. They drain the excess. Re-anchor the baselines. Restore truth to velocity. Because if motion isn't grounded, it's just spin. And when a project is burning hours but not burning scope, it is time for a mop check, a drain snake, and a flashlight under the sink.

The ambitious plan looked faultless. The tools were precision-grade, tested and certified by the best minds anywhere. But the mirror was wrong. Hubble's glass had passed inspection because the test used to verify it had quietly drifted off standard. The system trusted itself without realizing its own calibration had slipped. When the telescope launched, confidence filled the room. Then the images came back. The stars wouldn't focus. Nebulous. From orbit, there is no pulling over, no quick reset or hardware swap. But that is what had to happen. A mess written in the stars.

The Cleaning Strategy

NASA didn't replace the telescope. They didn't blame the team or rewrite history. They rolled up their sleeves and found the flaw. The mirror, ground too flat by just over two microns, was off by less than a strand of hair. But that sliver changed everything. Hubble could see, yes, but not clearly. Celestial bodies came back as blurs. What was meant to be revelation looked like devastation.

The problem certainly wasn't urgency. There was plenty of that. The problem was misguided trust. The kind without verification. The tool used to check the mirror had been assembled wrong. A single skewed spacer in the test rig convinced everyone the mirror was flawless. Once that belief took hold, no one challenged it. No one. Every report reinforced the mistake. Every sign-off locked it in. Hubble passed inspection because the measurement tool had slipped slightly out of spec, and that metric went unmonitored. This wasn't just a calibration issue. It was a failure to check the checker. A monitoring problem, plain and simple. Out of this world.

NASA didn't start over. They didn't replace the mirror. They built a workaround. Engineers designed a corrective optics package, essentially a pair of glasses for a ten-billion-dollar telescope and trained a shuttle crew to install it by hand. The device was called COSTAR. About the size of a phone booth, it used tiny mirrors to intercept and redirect the blurred light before it reached Hubble's cameras. Installation required five spacewalks, each one choreographed down to the fingerhold. The astronauts carried out the mission, but oversight of the cleanup belonged to the ground team. Strong minds, steady guidance, patient planning. The project janitor was never in the capsule. They were back on Earth, restoring vision for both the satellite and the project.

The Hubble repair was more than just a triumph of engineering. It was a masterclass in monitoring. The mirror had never changed. What changed was how the team looked at it. They questioned the assumption, traced the failure back to its point of origin, and realigned the system based on evidence, not belief. Fuzzy vision became clarity. Not through force, but through focus. That is the work of the project janitor. They don't start from scratch. They don't wait for disaster. They tune the instruments. They restore the standard. They make the project see itself clearly again. And when they're done, the mission doesn't just continue, everyone finally can see where it's going.

Scrub Away the Chaos

They stopped just outside the final village. The father placed the donkey's hooves back on the road, dusted off his sleeves, and looked at his son without speaking. They both knew. They had listened too long to the wrong signals. They had listened to the crowds when they should have simply kept walking. This time, they walked the rest of the way in silence. No spectacle. No burden. Just the two of them, steady beside the donkey, returning to the work of getting to their destination. And they did.

The Miller, His Son, and the Donkey. That's what true monitoring looks like. Not a dashboard or a meeting report, but a decision to stop chasing noise. The miller didn't call a meeting. He didn't escalate or replan. He simply set the donkey's hooves back on solid ground and walked forward with clarity. That moment, when the team stops reacting and starts observing, is when the project janitor's work unclogs the drain. It's the shift from presence to performance, from slippery motion to traction. Monitoring begins with the choice to see clearly. Just like NASA did.

Monitoring isn't about dashboards or reporting frequency alone. It's about knowing what to watch - and when. Project janitors don't track everything; they identify the signals that matter. Sometimes it's the lack of signals. They know which metrics tie directly to risk, which trends reflect schedule drift, and which behaviors indicate scope creep before it explodes. They set alerts where delays cascade. They run variance checks weekly to expose early signs of misalignment. They listen for silence where updates should be. They watch for blockers that don't move and deliverables that stay green without progress. They compare forecast to actuals, adjusting the mirror, to see clearly. Good monitoring means observing without interference and stepping in only when the pattern breaks. It's not surveillance. It's stewardship. Monitor the signals.

Lessons from the Janitor's Closet

The miller's mistake wasn't the donkey. It was listening too closely to every voice along the road. That's the risk in project monitoring: mistaking noise for a signal worthy of attention. A project janitor learns to filter the crowd, to stop pivoting with each opinion and start observing what matters. What small adjustment converts to impact. Monitoring doesn't mean changing course at every comment. People talk. Instead, the project janitor knows when the journey's still on track, even when others don't see it quite yet.

A single update won't tell the whole story. Repetition will. Missed milestones, vague standups, impediments that linger week to week without resolution. These aren't accidents. They're a pattern giving the blurry reality. The project janitor watches for what changes and what doesn't change. Drift is rarely dramatic at first. Divergence is subtle. That's why it matters to notice the slow, steady bends before they land you in the river.

Many blur the mirror between discussion and disposition. A noisy stakeholder doesn't mean the project is in trouble. A quiet one doesn't mean it's healthy. Project janitors don't monitor opinions, they monitor outcomes. They ground their observation in what's measurable: stories completed, scope burned, value delivered, tasks moved, risks addressed, clients satisfied. Reality speaks softly. But it always speaks. The job is to listen to it.

In complex projects, monitoring doesn't fail because no one cares. Often it fails because everyone assumes someone else is doing it. In one noteworthy Fortune 500 implementation, three experienced project managers split the lead. The structure looked sound. The resumes held weight. But what none of them claimed, what no one even discussed, was ownership of monitoring and control. What happened next wasn't dramatic. It was worse. It was believable.

Here's the story. The reporting structure was flat. Three project leaders, each senior, each autonomous. No single lead. No sequencing authority. No unified intake for scope changes, risk reviews, or delivery confirmation. Spreadsheets, here and there. Early on, it didn't matter. Kickoff went smoothly. Integration planning moved forward. The client was happy. Still, without one center of gravity, monitoring quickly splintered. Each project leader assumed the others were tracking the baselines. Each vendor worked from a slightly different schedule. The reports kept coming, but no one cross-checked them. Progress became red dressed in green's clothing.

The gaps showed up en masse. Not as errors, but as friction. A test case failed because the sales module didn't account for regional tax logic. Inventory looked synced until fulfillment flagged missing units. When integration teams finally compared notes, assumptions clashed. The plan had moved forward, but not together. The test team melted. What passed in isolation collapsed in sequence. One vendor flagged a billing dispute. Another stopped responding. What had looked like progress from afar now felt brittle up close. The project status shed its green exterior and went full-on red.

The response took time to coalesce. It was deeply fragmented, as were those running the project. One of the three project leaders quietly moved to a different initiative. No announcement. Simply reassignment.

The second buried himself in documentation, logging what had happened rather than changing what would. Monitoring using the rear view. The third became the voice to leadership, still framing updates in terms of percentage complete, still saying, "We're nearly there." No one addressed the gaps. No one owned the mirror. No matter. It was blurry anyway. The team kept working. The drift continued.

The project janitor arrived without a title change. No restructure. No announcement. Only presence. He didn't start with a dashboard or a replan. He asked a question. "Who owns the mirror?" The room went quiet. People looked around. Some chuckled. No one answered. He wasn't talking about a spreadsheet or a chart. He meant the mirror of monitoring. The place where percent complete has weight. Where scope burns, not just time. Where risk isn't tucked away. Where visibility is real, even when it's uncomfortable. And what did he find? The mirror wasn't broken after all. It had just been ignored. It needed to be fine-tuned.

He started at the edges. He activated the management's contingency fund, untouched until then. He brought in a forensic analyst to compare what the team had delivered against what the plan had promised. Not estimates, but evidence; earned value served as the measure. He set up a control room, both real and virtual, where dashboards pulled data from live sources and told the same story whether viewed from quality assurance or procurement. No more secret spreadsheets. No more selective visibility. He reviewed every work package. He assigned every ticket. He logged every change request and triaged every incident. The forgotten queue moved. Slowly at first. Then with intention. The image became clear.

Spills and Cleanup

The most dangerous projects aren't always the ones flashing red. They're the ones that stay green too long. Dashboards beam with color-coded confidence, but complaints rise. Status updates arrive on time but lack specifics. Teams adjust in isolation, quiet corrections made to meet expectations without disrupting the illusion of progress. We can round this, right? No one raises a flag, because no one wants to be first. By the time the project finally hits yellow or red, the mess is already stained into the foundation.

The project janitor doesn't wait for color changes. They look between the updates. A missing change request. A dependency that never quite aligns. A status line that says "on track" but leaves out the next milestone. Or the next. They listen to what's not said in standups. They notice when someone always answers second. When decisions get made in side threads. Elevator rides. When burndown rates stay linear but the team looks tired. These are the early signs. Before the dashboard blinks. Before divergence turns into collapse. Monitor to see the signs.

The breakdown of a project happens slowly. By slip. By deviation. Then one day the client asks why they haven't seen a sprint review in several iterations. The project janitor doesn't wait until the team can't explain why things no longer line up. They adjust early. By closely monitoring the project, they restore the feedback loops that were always supposed to be there. Not to control people, but to see clearly. Because once the mirror fogs, even the brightest star disappears. So, we fix it.

It's fixed beyond our wildest expectations.
-- Ed Weiler, Hubble Chief Scientist

Adding the Polish

Monitoring starts on day one and continues long after the crisis passes. It keeps the fix clean. Like checking a drain days after it's been cleared, the project janitor confirms that flow remains steady. People revert to old habits. Impediments happen. Mirrors fog. That's why the polish matters. Not for the shine, but for the inspection. Project janitors don't run reports because they're expected. They run them to verify that the recovery holds. It's not about checking the box. It's about checking the flow.

So, what is the polish? It's the quiet reinforcement of what was restored. Clarity. A cluttered dashboard is no more helpful than a blurry mirror. The project janitor standardizes reporting so teams and stakeholders work from the same source. They remove redundancy, align metrics to actual outcomes, and ensure every shared value has a clear, traceable origin. When done right, stakeholders stop asking for status because they can already see it. Transparency doesn't mean flooding the room with data. It means showing what matters, plainly and without distortion.

Adding the polish isn't about the shine. It's about confirmation. Project janitors verify that fixes hold under real conditions. They test not just functionality but trust, confirming that reports reflect reality, that schedules align with effort, and that no one hides risk behind optimism. For example, they may review closed items in the risk register or request post-launch validation to confirm that a feature is being used as intended. Such polish proves the system can hold under pressure. The inspection locks in the cleanup. It locks in the image. It worked for NASA. It works anywhere clarity matters. Once the plan reflects the work and the work reflects the truth, progress moves forward without second-guessing. Monitor. No guessing.

Janitor's Keyring

Don't confuse motion with progress. Trust what holds up under test. Focus the mirror not on speed alone, but on velocity. Velocity isn't just speed. It is anchored in direction. Adjust early. Verify the flow. The project janitor monitors what others overlook. That's how they clear the image. And how they keep it that way.

The Wisdom Within: The Miller, His Son, and the Donkey

A miller and his son set out for the market, walking beside their donkey. The plan was simple. The pace was steady.

Then a passerby scoffed. "You have a donkey and still you walk?" The son climbed aboard the animal. Seemed reasonable.

Moments later, another onlooker frowned. "A boy rides while his father walks? Disrespectful." They switched places. The father rode instead.

Further along, someone called out, "Why not both ride? It's faster." So many opinions. They adjusted again. Both climbed on.

Then came the next voice. "Two riders? That's cruel." So, they dismounted.

They realized, of course, that they were back where they started. Trying to get ahead of new criticism, they hoisted the donkey onto their shoulders. It seemed safer than being judged again.

But on the narrow bridge into town, the animal shifted its weight. The load tipped. The donkey fell. The load lost. They arrived at the market with no cargo, no outcome, and no plan.

Each reaction had made sense in the moment. Each adjustment had been small. But no one watched the direction. No one verified the load. No one monitored results against the plan. The mission slipped beneath the weight of every unfiltered opinion into nothing but blur.

-- Aesop, as told by a Project Janitor

Adding to Your Toolbox

Anchor the baseline: Begin every project by defining what real progress looks like. Align teams on specific outcomes, not just activity or perception.

PLAYBOOK FOR PROJECT JANITORS

Observe the rhythm: Spend time listening and watching how the work flows. Compare team behavior to the project plan. Look for signs that the two have drifted apart.

Notice early divergence: Track missed handoffs, vague updates, or shifting language. These are early indicators that progress is not aligned with the plan.

Verify actual progress: Do not rely on status reports alone. Check what has been delivered, confirm dependencies, and compare updates to what can be seen in the work itself.

Focus on the right signals: Monitor key indicators tied to schedule, scope, and risk. Set alerts for blockers. Review variance between planned and actual completion regularly.

Standardize visibility: Align dashboards, reports, and meeting updates to the same data. Remove duplicate sources and ensure everyone sees the same version of the truth.

Address misalignment early: When gaps appear, respond quickly. Revisit sequencing. Clarify ownership. Adjust schedules to match real conditions on the ground.

Sustain the fix: After the cleanup, continue monitoring. Verify that the recovery holds under pressure. Watch for slippage. Keep the mirror clear.

Chapter 12
Inspecting the Corners: Ensuring Quality Under Pressure

Executive Summary

This chapter tackles the hidden nature of quality and the quiet dangers that emerge when it's assumed instead of examined. The project janitor doesn't look for polish on the surface. They search for soundness in the structure. From system builds to construction sites, quality isn't a checklist. It's what endures under pressure. This chapter explores how unnoticed flaws, like a warped bell mold or a misaligned staging environment, can shape every outcome that follows. Through stories of ancient craftsmanship, real-world audits, and project recoveries, it shows how quality deviates when accountability fades and how the project janitor restores it by resetting expectations, slowing the pace, and confirming that each part can bear weight before the next one begins. Because when quality returns, it doesn't need to be declared. It rings true on its own.

The Mess at Hand

Every project has its cut corners. Edges no one checks. Handoffs no one questions. Outcomes assumed but never confirmed. Code untested. When speed becomes the mandate, quality becomes the casualty, not out of spite, but in the scramble to restore momentum. It often comes from the top: Get it done. So, the team moves faster. Trusts deeper. Races ahead on the strength of good intentions, believing someone else is checking the seams. But the truth of quality is quieter than confidence. It doesn't reveal itself in the demo. It hides in the depth, in how each piece connects, not just whether it works, but whether it endures.

Endurance can't be assumed. It must be examined. Yet too often, quality checks are treated as theater. Gated reviews passed with a glance. Test cases closed without full coverage. Peer signoffs issued in silence. The project marches on, propped up by paperwork instead of proof. "Done" gets declared by milestone, not by merit. Ask the team for their definition of done, and most will reach for the nearest checklist. But checklists don't catch echoes. They don't always test whether the work rings true. And without that test, a project can sound finished long before it's done.

You can feel it the moment you step in. The work looks completed. The documentation reads clean. The team says the right words. But the edge cases haven't been tested. The regression cycle was cut short. The quality assurance team is buried because the staging environment no longer reflects production. And no one can explain why the signoff happened when half the user stories changed. It doesn't look like a crisis. It's something quieter. A silent alarm, held in. A creeping confidence that quality has been covered, when truth doesn't prove it.

Eventually, the bell rings. A demo fails. A client clicks the one button no one tested. Blue screen. A report crashes, live, during a governance review. Is it data or code? Is it upstream or downstream? Is it even documented?

The breakdown doesn't derail the project, but it reveals the truth. The work that looked complete shows its gaps. The verification that should have happened gets exposed as guesswork. Trust doesn't dissolve. It recedes. And with it, the benefit of the doubt. From that point forward, every update draws scrutiny. Every green light invites suspicion. Because when quality breaks under pressure, the damage doesn't stop with delivery. It echoes in a relationship strained.

The same is true on the construction site: a concrete pour reveals that rebar was misaligned. The slab hardens before anyone notices. The structure might still stand, but now every next step demands review. Extra inspections. Delays. Defensive documentation. The cost isn't just time, it's trust lost, one layer below the surface.

This is the mess. Not just a failure of inspection, but a failure of quality itself. The team skipped controls. Leaders pushed early signoffs. Reviewers agreed without checking. They delivered what was asked, but not what was needed. Did what they were told, not what was right. The process rewarded progress over proof. The plan looked solid until pressure hit, and then it cracked. The client sounded the bell. No one can take back the echo. That is when the project janitor steps in to rebuild the checks that should have shaped the work from the start. Because quality, once questioned, doesn't repair itself. Someone must rebuild the path to confidence through clarity, through proper test cases, through follow-through. Only then does the ring sound true.

The Cleaning Strategy

Some failures stain the status report red. Obvious for all to see. Others wear a polished face and pass inspection. They slide through demos and peer reviews because the problems aren't loud. They're muted. A missing test. A bypassed step. A stale environment no one updated. Each miss takes up little space. So small, they hide just like the truth. No red flags. Just a quiet handoff, passed without question. Everyone trusts the last step. Everyone assumes the work is behind them. That's human nature. The point of the project is to finish. But if no one can label what "done" means, the job isn't really done. It's paused. Waiting to fail.

The project janitor doesn't audit the code or measure the tensile strength of the latest shipment of I-beams. They restore the structure that makes those checks possible. That starts with the test plan, not to glance at it, but to ask whether it reflects reality. Does it include regression? Was it updated after the last change? Then they move to the change log and look for signs of drift. Features marked complete without validation. Workarounds that became permanent. Deployments released without proof. They check the environments to confirm staging mirrors production and that someone owns that alignment. They carry a simple question: who is checking this now? Not who checked it before, or who meant to. Who owns it today. Because accountability fades fast, and when it does, quality follows.

The project janitor doesn't care if the project runs on code, copper, or concrete. They care whether it holds. The strategy? Widen the inspection in search of opportunities to improve quality. Check whether anyone tested the backup generator after the last outage. Whether the new process for vendor returns ever made it past the memo. Whether anyone walked the floor after the final punch list, or just clicked "complete." It's not about technology. It's about truth. Find it. The project janitor wants to see the real thing: working, failing, holding, breaking. Because quality doesn't live in status reports. It lives in what works when no one's watching.

The project janitor doesn't restore trust with promises. They restore it with proof. They don't assume a clean handoff from team to team. There are many silos. So, they verify. They trace each approval to an outcome, a measurable result, and make sure it holds. When needed, they slow the pace to expose what still needs attention. If something fails, they want it to fail here, now - not in front of the client. They tighten the space between assumption and evidence. They give the team a clear view of what still needs work and protect the time to do it. Because the next move isn't a guess. It's a commitment. And the project janitor doesn't let it go forward until it's ready to stand.

The bellmaker never got discouraged. He held back the villagers pausing for a quality product. When the bell finally rang, it worked as expected, it endured. No warble. No crack. Just a tone so clear it silenced the listeners in the square. No one asked who recast the mold or who realigned the strike plate. They only heard the result. A clean, lasting tone. And that was enough. The bellmaker never stepped forward. He just packed his tools and checked the next casting. The project janitor works the same way. They don't sign the quality report. They build the system that earns one. What holds under pressure doesn't need a hero. It rings true on its own.

Scrub Away the Chaos

The watchtower was mute. The first bell cracked. So did the second. Each one cast from the same mold, each one failing in the same way. The villagers didn't understand. They blamed the strike plate, the clapper, the tower itself. Every theory, every fix, every pour. None of it worked. The crowd grew restless. People shouted over one another. The square filled with noise, but not with the ring they longed to hear. That's the moment the bellmaker arrived. Quiet. Inspecting. Listening to the confusion echo louder than the bell ever had. The project janitor steps into this kind of mess every time. Not to explain the failure. To inspect the quality. Then adjust.

To scrub the chaos, the project janitor resets the pace. They stop the frantic patching and close the loop on unfinished work. They clear the schedule for an honest walkthrough. No slides. No summaries. Just the team, the build, and the plan side by side. A ride on the elevator, if you dare. Carry the blueprints and inspect the cables. Walk through test cases, punch lists, line by line. Mark gaps with tape and flag missed steps on the wall. Cross-check the materials list against what's real. If half the site says go and the other half waits for sign-off, the project janitor pulls everyone into one room. They delay the next release, if needed. Not to slow down development, but to protect the progress to come. Quality doesn't return through rework. It returns through verification and validation.

As the noise clears, the work speaks. Defects cluster in one corner of the process. Missed steps trace back to rushed reviews. The team sees it.

They stop guessing and correct the sequence. They bring issues forward and fix them without fear. Meetings shrink. Tasks get tested before they move. Deliverables match the plan. Reports become accurate. Each piece lines up because the project janitor made space for clarity to return. Because when the rhythm of work gets restored, so does the team's belief in what they build. Quality assured.

Lessons from the Janitor's Closet

The Parthenon still stands. Not only because it was grand but because it was corrected. The builders in Athens didn't just raise stone, they studied it. They walked the platforms, tested the joints, and adjusted every angle to deceive the eye toward beauty. Columns curve inward by design. The floor arcs ever so slightly. The corners sit tighter, thicker, more grounded. Not a single line is purely straight, because the human eye would misread it. Early engineers knew that. And they fixed it in advance. Under political pressure and on sacred ground, the work slowed for precision. The quality wasn't decorative. It was structural. What they delivered wasn't just a temple. It was a standard.

Parthenon flat lines seem to curve to the human eye. Straight columns bow. A perfect box looks hollow from a distance. The builders of the Parthenon understood this. They didn't fix flaws in the stone. They fixed flaws in perception. What looked symmetrical on parchment distorted in the sun. A level floor seemed to sag. Equal spacing between columns appeared uneven once raised against the sky. Without correction, the temple would stand, yes, but it would never look right. And the Athenians weren't building for utility. They were building for the divine. They wanted the gods to see harmony. They wanted future generations to see order. That meant correcting for what the eye would lie about. That meant building something that felt true, even if it wasn't purely geometric.

Every correction cost them time. The treasury strained. Voices in the Assembly pushed for speed. But the builders held their ground. They cut and recut marble not because the first stone was damaged, but because the monument could be better. They filed the joints so precisely that mortar was optional. They adjusted angles until shadows fell evenly across the flutes of each column. They kept walking the perimeter, checking the alignment against both plan and perception. They knew the stone would settle. They knew heat would shift it. So, they built in tension, curvature, and lift. The columns leaned not because of failure, but because of foresight. And when the temple opened, no one noticed the corrections. They saw harmony. Quality.

Spills and Cleanups

Quality doesn't always collapse with a beam of bent light. But the illusion is the same. It started with a routine audit, 2012. A Fortune 100 manufacturer wanted to tighten financial controls and check the stability of its pricing and payment systems across global regions. The project seemed simple: confirm policies, review workflows, reinforce standards. But the deeper they looked, the less their process held. Pricing rules shifted between departments. Return handling varied by region. Approvals were unclear. Data didn't match.

No one had noticed. Not because the problems were hidden, but because no one was looking from the center. Too many silos. Each team trusted their own slice. But quality lagged. Controls stretched. The company's 120-day audit requirement had lost its grip. Some followed it loosely. Some not at all. There were no bells, no red flags, only quiet variations. That's how most quality failures begin.

They brought in an external audit consulting team. Not to fix the numbers, but to examine the system. The team didn't assume risk lived only in obvious places. They expanded their scope to include regions no one had ever questioned. They traced every approval path. They reviewed real transactions. What they found was divergence in all functions of the business. Vendor terms didn't match payments. Desktop spreadsheets had replaced systems of record. Roles blurred. Quality had stopped being enforced and started being assumed.

The recovery began by putting checks where they mattered. Pricing approvals. Return verifications. Contract terms. These controls were tied to real steps in the workflow, not as rework, but as prevention. The audit became more than a report. It became a feedback loop. Quality didn't just return. It reconnected to the work itself.

Twelve million dollars returned in the first cycle. One hundred and ten million over time. But the recovery wasn't just financial. What proved it was the shift. Teams no longer had to ask if the process worked. They could see it in the flow, the results, the clarity. Quality didn't just return. It became the standard.

Quality means doing it right when no one is looking.
-- Henry Ford

Adding the Polish

The project janitor doesn't announce that quality has returned. They let the work reveal it. The signs vary by project, but the truth stays the same. In a system, it's the test that passes the first time. In a walk-through, it's the absence of surprises. In software, it's the deployment that doesn't need rollback. When the test environment matches production without excuse. When regression covers the full sequence, including the edge cases. On a construction site, it's the wiring that clears on first inspection. The punch list that shrinks from real completion, not shortcut. This isn't polish for presentation. It's polish that confirms the repair. The precision of the build. The quiet of a clean test cycle. The approval given through proof, not assumption. These aren't signs of luck. They're the result of follow-through.

Polish makes quality obvious. It shows in posture. The client no longer asks for reassurance. The team doesn't second-guess what's complete. The questions elevate. They move from "Did we remember this?" to "What else can we improve?" That's what polish returns: a working rhythm, rooted in alignment. Continuous improvement. You hear it in the way people speak. You see it in how they move. Quality becomes the ring from the watchtower again.

The polish that matters doesn't simply decorate the surface. It confirms the foundation. Not perfect, proven. The project janitor isn't there to impress. They're there to complete, with quality. They leave when the structure answers for itself. That's why their work remains. Not because someone said it was done, but because every part stands on its own. Ready. Reliable. Done right. Even when no one is looking.

Janitor's Keyring

Quality isn't found on a checklist. It's what holds its shape and endures under pressure. Like the Parthenon, the work lasts not because it looked right from one point of view, but because it was studied from every angle and adjusted where it fooled the eye. The project janitor brings that same lens, checking the taper, testing the assumptions, and confirming that the structure stands. Complete, aligned, and able to bear weight without question.

The Wisdom Within: The Bellmaker's Secret

There was once a village with a watchtower on its highest ridge. For generations, a bell had hung there, a warning bell, cast to carry across the hills in case of fire, flood, or attack. When the old bell cracked with age, the village gathered its best metalsmiths to forge a new one. They melted bronze, poured it into the same mold, and raised the bell into the tower. It looked perfect. Polished. Symmetrical.

But when they struck it, the sound fell flat. A dull tone. A wobble. Dampened. Incomplete. Something was wrong.

They blamed the clapper and replaced it. Still wrong. They adjusted the strike. Reinforced the beam. Poured another bell from the same mold. It cracked too as did the third. Each failure brought more noise, arguments, accusations, guesswork disguised as solutions. The villagers grew frustrated. Some wanted to blame the tower. Others said the mountain air was too thin. A few insisted the bell was fine, and the listeners were the problem.

Still, the bell would not ring true.

One morning, an old bellmaker arrived. He listened. Not just to the tone, but to the silence between tones. He climbed the tower. Tapped the metal. He didn't rush. After much thought, he asked a simple question: had anyone examined the mold itself?

They had not.

So, he scraped it clean. Held a straightedge to the curve. He found what others missed, an imperceptible warp in the casting form. Just a few degrees off. Enough to bend the shape, distort the tone, and cause the same failure every time. He recast the mold, adjusted the angle, thickened the lip. And poured metal just one more time.

When the new bell rang, it rang clean. True. No warble. No crack. Just clarity. The crowd fell silent. The sound commanded it.

The bellmaker did not take credit. He packed his tools and left before the echo faded.

That's what the project janitor notices first. Not the crowd. Not the blame. The broken mold. The quiet flaw that shaped every outcome after it. They don't patch failures or reframe the message. They check the form. The assumptions baked into process. The approvals cast from habit. They look for the place where quality drifted, not in the visible work alone, but in the structure that formed it. Then they recast. They shore up the mold. Because in projects, as in bell towers, what lasts isn't the ring. It's the shape that makes it possible.

-- Project Janitor

Adding to Your Toolbox

Confirm the baseline: Begin by verifying what "done" actually means for each workstream. Do not assume that definitions are shared across teams.

Check the mold: Look beyond the surface. Examine the underlying structure, plan, or process that is shaping the deliverables. If the source is off, the results will follow.

Reset the pace: If work has been rushed, pause the cycle. Make time for walkthroughs, hands-on testing, and full inspections across environments and teams.

Walk the floor: Conduct live reviews. Ride the elevator. Test the build. Match what is documented against what actually exists.

Trace approvals: Confirm that every signoff links to a verified outcome, not just a completed checkbox. Look for drift where assumptions replaced validation.

Inspect edge cases: Extend quality checks beyond the happy path. Run regression tests. Confirm that staging mirrors production. Test what others skip.

Tighten the gap: Close the distance between assumption and evidence. Do not move forward until the work holds up to inspection under real conditions.

Protect the work: Slow the next release if needed. Make space for corrections before they harden into larger failures downstream.

Standardize follow-through: Establish visible, repeatable checks. Align the team on which steps are mandatory before delivery.

Let quality prove itself: Do not declare the fix. Let it be confirmed through reduced defects, cleaner reviews, and work that holds its shape under pressure.

Chapter 13
Recovering a Slippery Start: Containing the Spill and Owning the Origins

Executive Summary

Projects don't fail at the finish line, they fail long before, quietly. Not with a bang, but a slow, unnoticed deviation from the plan. This chapter explores how misalignment, overlooked signs, and premature trust lead to systemic breakdowns that appear sudden, but aren't. The project janitor doesn't wait for failure to announce itself. They study the early warnings, the slow leaks, the unasked questions. This isn't just about fixing what slipped. It's about recognizing what allowed the slip in the first place.

Through stories of failed pumps, collapsed bridges, and cracked water jars, Chapter 13 shows that project recovery isn't just containment. It's accountability, insight, and inspection. Not everything broken needs to be replaced. But everything trusted must be verified. The project janitor brings presence, steadiness, and clarity to restore not only the flow, but the system that holds it.

The Mess at Hand

Some spills don't start with a deluge but a trickle. They start with overconfidence. Signed agreements. Green dashboards. High-level nods. Everything looks aligned until the project turns hamster and rides the wheel. Motion without movement. The dashboard turns red. What appeared stable was already slipping. This didn't happen without divergence. What slipped was already compromised. The Mess at Hand isn't about emergency response. It's about recognizing that most project emergencies don't begin where the eruption dumps its lava. They begin earlier. Quieter. When someone says, "good enough," before verifying anything is "done right."

You arrive late. You always do, by janitorial design. The spill has already reached the carpet, soaked into the wiring, warped the framing no one thought to seal. The schedule's slipping, but no one said anything until the contractor stopped answering calls. The statement of work is missing a clause. Okay, many. The ticketing system was never updated. And the assumptions at kickoff, spoken with certainty by those in charge, never recorded the decisions. Now the project sponsor wants containment. The vendor wants forgiveness. And the team just wants clarity. But what they need first is presence. Yours.

This isn't new. It's just unspoken. The project didn't slip yesterday. It drifted quietly, over weeks, maybe months. A missed dependency here. A milestone passed with no deliverable. Okay, many. Risk logs with no risks. No risks? Everyone stayed optimistic, because no one wanted to be the one to interrupt momentum. And now that motion has hardened into misalignment. The team still moves, but no one is sure whether they're moving forward. Burning hours without burning scope. This is the moment when someone calls it urgent. But it wasn't speed that caused the mess. It was silence. No one owned it.

When the project janitor arrives, the question isn't "What's broken?" It's "What was already broken before anyone noticed?" Not just the symptom, but the systemic cause. Not just the missed date, but the assumptions beneath it. The project janitor doesn't chase chaos. They study it. Carefully. They ask why the scope was assumed, why the schedule was rushed, why the risk register read empty for six straight months. Most of all, they ask why no one else asked. Because the real spill isn't the water on the floor. It's the crack that let it in. Recognize the crack.

The problem isn't that spills happen. Of course they do. The problem is that no one checks the seal. No one notices a change in rhythm. No one sees the drip. Until it pools. Until it twists steel. Until the pump is lost. By then, the system has already failed. And everyone knows. The contract is still active, the milestone is still labeled green, but stakeholders can feel the wobble. They hear the clatter. That's when the project janitor steps in, not to point fingers, but to assess, adjust, and stabilize. They don't ask who cracked the jar. They carry the patch kit. They're going to need it.

Own a pool? You'll recognize this project spill. It starts with silence. No alarms sound. No one heard the impeller jam. The motor hum. The switch trip. Then nothing. You don't get called when all systems are nominal. You get called when they're stalled. When the pump was supposed to self-prime, but didn't. So, you check. You open the casing. You find buildup where there should have been clearance. Saltwater? Yes. A trace of salt. A notch in the seal. A shaft that should have been protected, but wasn't. No O-ring? The system was never truly aligned. It just ran well enough not to raise concern, until it didn't. And now it needs more than motion. It needs replacement. Still, the project janitor is not here to restore flow but to restore what allows it.

Some projects are bridges over water. Some are busted pool pumps. This one may not span the bay, but in the moment, it holds the same weight: expectation, structure, trust. Overheated kids. The replacement isn't rushed. It's deliberate. The project janitor pulled the old motor out stiff and stained. The shaft was scored. The seal brittle. The impeller frozen in place. Where is that O-ring? There never was one. Newly installed by the dealer, it moved water anyway, for a few months, just long enough to keep the pool blue. But that's the danger. When shortcuts spin without noise, they earn a false confidence. And then they stop. When they shouldn't. That's the spill. Let's clean it up.

The Cleaning Strategy

Replace the motor not the pool. The new motor seats with precision, not because the design was flawless, but because this time the work is. You clean the shaft. Free the impeller. Grease and set the seal. By the book, no guesswork. You run a proper ground. You take no chances. The original build ran just long enough to earn trust, but not long enough to deserve it. That's the danger with shallow motion. It hides the absence of alignment. Until the whole system stops.

This is where strategy begins. Not with status meetings or slide decks, but with attention. Physical, grounded, present. You don't replace the whole system. You fix what failed, and what let it fail. One motor, not the whole pool. One wire. One fitting. One page of documentation that should have existed and now will. Project cleanup doesn't begin at the top. It begins at the threads. The overlooked. The misaligned. The unrecorded.

The motor is new, but it doesn't live alone. Cleanup doesn't end at replacement. It extends outward. The pump. The water lines. The pad beneath the frame. You check each one. You test every assumption the last installer left behind. You trace the shortcuts that brought it to this eventuality. That's strategy. Not just velocity, but careful inspection. The project janitor doesn't assume anything downstream is clean just because upstream now hums. They follow the system to its edges. That's how you prevent the next spill. And this strategy works for all projects.

There's a story about a cracked jar, sent each morning to carry water from a spring. By the time it reached home, half the water was gone. The jar apologized. It had failed, it said. But the water bearer smiled and pointed to the path. Flowers had bloomed where the leak had passed. The jar wasn't perfect, no, but it had delivered more than it knew.

That's the thing about cleanup. You don't just replace what's broken. You study what broke. You learn when the damage happened and what it still managed to support. You notice what grew in the cracks. Because sometimes, a project survives not despite the spill, but because of what it forced into the light. Damage isn't just something to fix. It's something to learn from. Don't replace the whole pool. Unless you must.

Scrub Away the Chaos

They called it Galloping Gertie. The Tacoma Narrows Bridge wasn't a disaster waiting to happen. It was a marvel, until it wasn't. When it opened in 1940, it spanned the Puget Sound with grace. Light, elegant, and modern. But when the wind came, it didn't shake. It swayed. It twisted. It rippled like a ribbon. The engineers had calculated weight, load, tension. But they hadn't accounted for resonance. Oscillation. The bridge didn't collapse from weight, it collapsed from instability.

That's what makes some spills so dangerous. They don't start with force. They start with motion. Beautiful, believable motion. A system that looks elegant from the outside, even while its core alignment is off by a fraction, unfortunately, just enough. A bridge tuned to its own undoing. A project where no one speaks up when the schedule flexes just a little, or where requirements shift in small, agreeable ways. It all feels smooth, until the oscillation takes hold. Until good intentions start reinforcing the wrong pattern. And by the time someone calls for help, it's not just the plan that's twisting. It's the structure beneath it.

The project janitor didn't design the bridge. They weren't at the ribbon cutting. They weren't consulted when the wind patterns were logged or the cables selected. But when the shaking started, Washington State leaders called. The project janitor arrived not with fanfare, but with a notebook. They watched. They listened. They didn't silence the motion. They studied its frequency. The task wasn't to stop the swaying. It was to understand what allowed it, what reinforced it, what had never been tested. That's what a project janitor does when chaos starts to ripple the structure. They don't brace it. They find the fault where the misalignment began. Find the fault.

The engineers weren't careless. They were precise. They did what they knew how to do, and at the time, the Tacoma Narrows Bridge was considered advanced. It met all standards. The math checked out. The materials were sound. Still, some forces don't show up in a formula. Not until they appear in motion. Aerodynamic resonance wasn't fully understood in 1940. No one ignored the risk. They just didn't know it was there. That's the reality behind some of the worst failures. The unknown. Not neglect. Just an assumption left untested, reinforced by progress that looked smooth. Until.

Cleanup didn't mean replicating the same bridge with bigger beams. It meant starting over with better questions. Modern civil engineering was born. The new design wasn't just stronger. It was smarter. Wider decks. Open trusses. Wind tunnels and modeling that hadn't existed before. The collapse didn't just mark the end of a bridge. It marked the beginning of a new understanding. That's a flower blooming where the leak had passed.

That's what the project janitor restores. Not the structure, but the insight it lacked. They don't rebuild to soothe fear. They rebuild to correct the cause. Because overcorrection can be its own failure. It often is. Replace what failed. Study what allowed it. Preserve what held. Don't redesign just to get the project back under control. Redesign for clarity. When alignment fails, recovery isn't about going back. It's about building forward. Thoughtfully. Don't replace the whole bridge. Unless you must.

Lessons from the Janitor's Closet

Emergencies never begin in the moment they're declared. They have already unfolded with a hush. A skipped check. A risk unlogged. A seal that's almost good enough. The failure is already in motion, just not yet visible. By the time the motor stalls or the bridge sways, the system has been out of alignment for too long. That's the truth a project janitor learns to see. The mess isn't sudden. It's slow. It's quiet. And it's preventable, if someone is looking early enough.

Alignment isn't guaranteed by activity. The system may move, but that doesn't mean it's on the right path. Projects drift when no one checks the tracks the work rests on. When the shaft spins, but no one checks the seal. When the schedule moves, but no one confirms deliverables. We must contain the spill and own the origin. The project janitor doesn't assume momentum means progress. They test the system. They verify what others only passively view. That's how alignment is recovered, by measuring what supports the movement, not just admiring the motion.

Ownership doesn't cast blame. It forges presence, attention. The project janitor steps in not to defend the plan or rewrite the past, but to take responsibility. Accountability. For what comes next. The ownership is extreme. Swords standing by. That's the turning point. Accountability owned. It doesn't matter who caused the spill, but who contains it. Not who missed the risk, but who sees it now and moves. Cleanup *without* ownership is surface work. But cleanup *with* ownership changes the outcome. It restores more than alignment. It restores trust. Integrity.

Ownership brings weight. But the project janitor doesn't carry it alone. They use it to steady the team. Not by correcting every detail, but by restoring direction. Divergence happens when people keep moving without remembering where they're headed. The project janitor doesn't impose the plan. They reconnect the work to its purpose. They anchor the team, not to the scope itself, but to scope understood through clarity. Progress isn't about doing more. It's about aligning what's already in motion. Align.

Spills and Cleanup

There was no early warning system. No reliable forecast model. The metrics were reported, but not believed. The project didn't fall behind at the deadline. It stalled long before, quietly, invisibly. The due date wasn't the problem. It was the stillness that led to it. That's what the project janitor inherits. Not just delay, but disconnection. Silence. Learn to read it. It's not just a spill, but the absence of warning. And once the stall becomes visible, panic rushes in to fill the space where planning should have been. But panic is a poor substitute. Cleanup begins with presence, not urgency. With facts, not fury. A reset, not a reaction. Because in the end, what failed wasn't the timeline. It was the trust in the system built to watch it.

The surprise wasn't the delay. It was that no one saw it coming. Reports were filed. Checkpoints passed. But deliverables weren't confirmed. Conversations drifted from facts to feelings. From outcomes to optics. The project looked healthy until it didn't, because no one verified the warning beneath the status. A green light doesn't turn red without passing through yellow, but someone has to care to pay attention. Cleanup means reading the pattern before it hardens. Knowing that the moment a project "feels off," it likely already is. Don't wait for failure to confirm what silence has already screamed.

The spill isn't always in the code or the concrete. Sometimes it's in the calendar. The approval cycle. The contract clause everyone read but no one understood. A forgotten dependency. An unvalidated estimate. The project janitor doesn't panic when these appear. They reestablish rhythm. Find the beat the team lost. Spills can't be reversed. But they can be contained. Mop handy? That's cleanup. Naming what slipped. Realigning the goal. Turning the unknown into knowns, fast. Because the only thing worse than a slipped date is steadying the project, only to watch the target push to the right again.

Context matters. But the cleanup stops with the one still holding the mop.
-- Project Janitor

Adding the Polish

The new bridge didn't rise out of shame. It rose out of careful study. The failure didn't erase the work. It revealed the edge of what was known. And from that edge, something stronger had to grow. That's what the project janitor polishes. They start at the surface, then press deep into the lesson. Not to shine it, but to understand it. What they leave behind isn't just a fix. It's a system better prepared. A team better tuned. Insight that holds where the crack once was, not to impress, but to prevent. Because even a collapsed bridge leaves a lesson plan behind it, if you know how to follow it.

The bridge fell. The pump ceased. The jar leaked. Still, none of these events defined the outcome. What did was what happened next. Remember? All that matters now is what we do next. Study. Repair. Purpose. Cleanup isn't measured in motion but in what endures after it. It's not about removing every flaw. It's about making sure the same flaw doesn't return disguised as progress. The project janitor doesn't aim for perfection. They aim for resilience.

Because at the end of it, someone still has to walk the path, carry the water, test the current, and cross the span. The cleanup isn't done when the system runs. It's done when the cracks are understood, the alignment is confirmed, and the work can move forward without rebreaking the seal. That's the polish. Not decoration. Not theater. Just what's left when every unnecessary thing is wiped away.

Janitor's Keyring

The project janitor doesn't clean up the spills to rewrite the stories. They steady what slipped, restore what holds, and leave behind a system that no longer hides its cracks. Alignment returns not through urgency, but through attention. Quiet. Grounded. Complete. That's the key they carry.

The Wisdom Within: The Cracked Jar at the Spring

There was once a water bearer who worked for a quiet household on a hill. Each morning, she walked down the path to the spring, balancing a wooden pole across her shoulders. On either end hung a large clay jar. One jar was flawless. Smooth, symmetrical, and whole. The other was cracked, with a thin fracture running down its side.

By the time the water bearer returned to the house each day, the perfect jar remained full. The cracked jar had leaked half its contents. This went on for months.

One morning, the cracked jar spoke.

"I'm sorry," it said. "I know I've failed. I lose water every day. You work so hard, but I can't deliver as much as the other jar."

The woman smiled. "Look behind us," she said.

The jar turned to see the path they had walked. It was lined with blossoms. Bright flowers blooming only on the cracked jar's side.

"I knew about your crack," the woman said. "So, I planted seeds on your side of the path. And each day as we walked back, you watered them. I gathered them for the vase. They've brought color and life to this place. You haven't failed. You've grown something no other jar ever could."

The cracked jar didn't hold the full measure. But it delivered something unexpected. Not despite the flaw. Because of it.

That's the project janitor's journey. Not all spills ruin the work. Some reveal the system. Some feed the path. Not every loss is failure. Sometimes it is redirection. A flawed implementation, a slipped date, a missed connection. Each can carry lessons forward if you choose to follow the trail.

What matters isn't whether the jar was perfect. What matters is what bloomed along the way. Don't replace the jar.
-- Traditional folktale, as told by a Project Janitor

Adding to Your Toolbox

Arrive: Step in without blame. Let your focus and steadiness signal that containment has begun.

Ask what allowed the spill: Go beyond what slipped. Identify the misalignment, silence, or shortcut that made failure possible.

Find the origin: Trace each issue to its root. Not the symptom, but the first unverified assumption or overlooked risk.

Test the system: Do not assume the rest of the structure holds. Verify dependencies, approvals, and connections before restarting flow.

Contain before correcting: Stop further damage first. Bring the motion under control before planning the recovery.

Repair deliberately: Replace what failed with care. Clean the process, reset expectations, and align the team before resuming work.

Follow the fault line: After the repair, widen your inspection. Study what else drifted silently. Don't trust what hasn't been tested.

Reestablish rhythm: Restore direction through cadence. Reconfirm the next steps and timelines once the team is grounded again.

Document what changed: Capture the realignment. Turn guesswork into clarity and restore confidence in the path forward.

Learn from the fracture: Reflect on what was revealed. Let the insight shape future planning and prevent recurrence.

Preserve what held: Not everything failed. Acknowledge the elements that endured and carry them forward.

Own the cleanup: Take accountability for recovery. What matters now is not who cracked the jar, but who steadied the system after.

ð. Ciarcia Jr., PMP, PJ

Chapter 14
Buffing Away Resistance: Change That Holds Without Force

Executive Summary

This chapter explores the art of organizational change through the quiet strength of influence. Project janitors don't demand alignment. They invite it. They don't shout over the noise; they adjust the rhythm beneath it. Real transformation doesn't begin with mandates or metrics. It begins when teams feel safe enough to follow and confident enough to continue, without being pushed, pulled, poked, or dragged.

Through field-tested practice, this chapter shows how cleanup becomes contagious when the new way feels like the better way. Not louder. Not harsher. Just clearer. Cleaner. Chosen. Project janitors don't herd cats. They walk a path the cats want to follow. They simplify what's cluttered, highlight what's working, and let the rhythm carry forward on its own. Because in real change, the goal is never to control the crowd. It is to help them hear the tune and walk in time.

The Mess at Hand

Some messes resist cleanup not because they're buried, but because they've been there so long no one sees them anymore. Olfactory adaptation. Habits form. Workarounds calcify. Teams inherit processes like oversized, outdated, and frayed hand-me-down coats and still wear them beyond usefulness because change feels colder than the flaws they already know. Resistance isn't always ominous. Sometimes it's polite. It shows up, signs off, then drifts quietly back to the way things were. What you're cleaning up isn't just a project. It's the residue of comfort, tradition, and fear.

You can spot it when every improvement feels temporary. When pilot programs stall after the champion leaves. When legacy tools outlive their usefulness by five versions and three reorgs but still occupy center stage because no one wants to challenge the past. No eye contact. The problem isn't always the plan. It's the adoption. The resistance. The quiet undoing. What you inherit isn't just technical debt. It's emotional debt. Process familiarity. A learned aversion to new promises. Fear. And until you name that, until you acknowledge the resistance as part of the mess, you're not cleaning. You're just playing another game of mahjong.

That's why organizational change management doesn't start with staff memos. It starts with cleanup. Not of the system but of the story. Cultural sediment. You strip away the narratives that say the old way is safer. That the new way was tried and failed. That managing adoption is someone else's job. Because as long as those stories stay lodged in the corners, the trash doesn't leave. It just gets sorted. Stacked. Named something respectable and left in place. Legacy.

Some teams polish what they refuse to replace. They redesign the dashboard, but not the business logic. They rebrand the workflow but never reexamine its purpose. The result looks better. Cleaner. Diagrammed. But they don't improve the process. It doesn't scale or adapt. And when it fails to deliver, they blame the users. Or the tools. Or the timing. Anything but the hollowness underneath. Because to admit it looked right but lacked substance, stings. For project janitors, that's the real cleanup. The kind that can't be delegated.

The Cleaning Strategy

Begin with this: Don't fight the resistance. Sweep around it. That's where the real work starts. Most change efforts fail not because the change is flawed, but because the resistance is misunderstood. It isn't about sabotage. It's about keeping the familiar. Routine. Sometimes comfortable. Sometimes built from layoffs after the last transformation. From upgrades that downgraded usability. From leaders who promised a better way, then vanished before it stuck. Sometimes it's a fear of the new. Sometimes it's a fear of looking unskilled in front of peers. Of losing control. Or of learning something that makes you question years of mastery.

Resistance isn't a barrier. It's a buildup. And project janitors don't pound it until it splatters everywhere. They loosen it, bit by bit, until it can be cleared. You listen first. Not for what's said in meetings, but for what's muttered in hallways. That's where the real stories live. You'll hear that the last system was supposed to save time. Then it added steps. That a former director pushed automation, then left a manual workaround. That someone got punished for raising a concern. Now they want an opinion? None of these issues show up on the roadmap. But they shape every footstep toward change. Project janitors don't just push the tools they are brought in to deploy. They sweep the floor for buried stories that explain why no one's following.

You'll also find resistance dressed up as refinement. The process has a name, a diagram, a formal release. It looks official. But no one uses it. Or they use just enough of it to say they did. That's when you know you're dealing with a mask. Polished on the outside. Hollow behind the eyes. The cleanup here isn't physical. It's perceptual. You're not removing clutter. You're removing the illusion that something valuable is already in place.

The hardest part isn't spotting the mask. It's helping the team see that it doesn't fit. That the process they're following was built for a different time, a different scale, a different need. The mask once matched the face. Now it slips. It pinches. It hides more than it helps. And the longer it stays on, the harder it is to speak clearly. The project janitor doesn't rip it off. They hold up a mirror. They help the team see that the current state isn't just flawed, it's no longer theirs.

That's the cleanup strategy. Not enforcing change, but inviting it. Quiet pilots. Shadow rollouts. Small spaces where people can try the new way without the weight of ceremony. No mandates. Just movement. A rhythm they recognize. You don't push. You play the tune. Let the team follow it through the old alleyways, past habits and hesitations. On a software project, it might be a soft launch, a workflow walk-through, or a focus group previewing the training path. In construction, it might be a single site supervisor walking the revised safety sequence before the morning pour, or piloting the new tool check-out routine for one crew. You let them find where it flexes and where it fails. And when they spot the improvements themselves, adoption follows. Not because it was required, but because it felt natural. Owned. The cleanup sticks when the path feels like one they chose.

But even the best tune fades if it's not echoed. You can't play once and walk away. You circle back. You listen for rhythm in their steps. Has it taken root? Or are they humming it only when you're nearby? Because change doesn't hold just because it started well. It holds when it's repeated. When it sings on its own. When the new way gets reinforced in meetings, in metrics, in small wins that become shared stories. The project janitor's fife doesn't disappear. It gets passed along. Until the team is playing it themselves.

That's what the cleanup strategy delivers. Not just a cleaner process, but a quieter resistance. One that has been heard. Dismantled. Rewritten. The project janitor does more than just sweep up the mess. They reset the rhythm. The steps ahead have traction. Participation. The old path fades, not because it was forced aside, but because something better took its place and earned attention. And the tune that led them there? It doesn't need to be played forever. Just long enough for the team to carry it on their own. Be the pied piper.

Scrub Away the Chaos

Scrubbing away the chaos begins with cats. You know the kind. The teams that scatter when it's time to align. That paw at new tools, then nap in the old ones. Each with their own habits, their own flavor of process pride. They aren't malicious. Just independent. Restless. Overfed on past initiatives and underwhelmed with change. The project janitor doesn't chase them. Doesn't trap or prod. They play the tune. A rhythm simple enough to follow. Familiar enough to try. And if the cleanup works, the cats believe it was their idea all along.

You don't scrub chaos by issuing commands. You do it by lowering defenses. By clearing space. One shared folder becomes the source. One dashboard becomes the truth. One step removed, not twelve added. The goal isn't to standardize everything but to reduce friction until teams start to move. Willingly. You're not forcing alignment. You're making it easier than divergence. And in that stillness, they follow. Not because they were told to. Because suddenly, the mess is harder to justify than the change.

You don't scrub chaos by dragging people until they resist. Or poking them until change is painful. Or pushing until trust breaks. That's how cats scatter. That's how teams retreat. The project janitor plays it differently. A tune. A rhythm. A pace that feels chosen. Let the new pattern echo until it settles. Quiet wins. Shared language. Fewer questions in standups, more movement on the floor. That's when you know the chaos has cleared. Not when the cats are counted, but when they stop looking for the exit. You don't lead by force. You lead by allowing them to make the path their own. Because the job was never to drive them. It was to help them walk in time. To guard the new rhythm. To accept the change.

Lessons from the Janitor's Closet

Even excellence gets messy. In the early 2000s, Toyota, the gold standard of lean manufacturing, found itself slipping. Rapid expansion, growing complexity, and a wave of public recalls revealed a deeper mess. Quality controls had blurred. Local plants had drifted from core principles. The culture that once prized continuous improvement had begun to stall. A company built to eliminate waste had become bloated with process. Layers of approvals. Legacy reports. Habits defended with new titles. Success filled the room. But it hadn't been cleaned. And when the spotlight hit, the dust showed.

This wasn't just a technical failure. It was cultural clutter. Toyota's DNA, once rooted in daily reflection and frontline ownership, had started to erode. As the company scaled globally, its practices scattered. Local offices clung to rituals but lost the reason behind them. Kaizen became ceremony. Gemba became symbolic. Reviews became rituals. Processes that once evolved through scrutiny were now laminated and left untouched. And when internal corrections were suggested, resistance didn't roar. It shrugged. The habits had hardened. The system wasn't broken in parts. It was stale. All of it.

The cleanup didn't begin with restructuring. It began with reawakening. Toyota didn't hire outsiders to fix the mess. They turned inward. Back to the floor. Back to gemba, where the real issues emerge, as do the people who solve them. Senior leaders walked the plants. They listened. Not to metrics or reports, but to frontline rhythm. Where friction built. Where process frayed. Where trust thinned. There were no slogans. No reset banners. Just presence. Humility. A willingness to see what had been missed. Because before you change anything, you have to admit what no longer works. And that's not a leadership summit. That's a broom in hand.

Then they acted. They didn't just reorganize. They threw out the trash. Outdated reports no one read. Shadow tools that duplicated effort behind the scenes. Binders full of procedures no one used but everyone defended. At Toyota, cleanup became culture. Through the 5S system - Sort, Set in Order, Shine, Standardize, Sustain - they didn't just rearrange clutter. They removed it. Visibly. Relentlessly. They swept floors and cleared closets. But they also eliminated status meetings that had lost purpose and templates that blocked real thinking. Waste wasn't just material. It was procedural. And by throwing it out in the open, they gave others permission to do the same. Order followed not because it was imposed, but because it was revealed.

This wasn't a mandate. It was music. Leaders didn't launch 5S with banners or speeches. They showed up early and began clearing space. No ceremony. Simply sleeves rolled. Everyone did the work. The message didn't travel in memos. It moved through motion. Deliberate. Repeatable. Relief returned. The rhythm of change moved from leadership to the floor. Not prescribed, but echoed. Like a tune that lingered until you found yourself humming it. And once they did, they didn't stop. Not because they were told to. Because they finally saw what was possible. The cleanup wasn't handed down. It was passed along.

The cleanup didn't stall with leadership. It multiplied. Line leads reorganized tool boards without a memo. Floor teams questioned inventory signals they used to ignore. The old patterns lost their grip. Not because they were banned, but because better ones had taken hold. Everyone knew. What began as misperception became alignment. The rhythm caught. And when someone adjusted a layout or retired a useless chart, it didn't feel like rebellion. It felt like clarity. That's how the real cleanup spreads. When alignment feels less like compliance and more like a shared decision.

The lesson at Toyota didn't end with cleaner plants. It ended with stronger teams. What they swept away wasn't just dust or documents. It was resignation. The quiet kind that settles in when change feels imposed, not chosen. By turning cleanup into cadence, by making clarity a shared act, they didn't just recover performance. They recovered trust. Honorably. That's the work of the project janitor. Not to impose the change, but to start the rhythm so others can carry it forward, making it stick because it's theirs. Start the rhythm.

Spills and Cleanup

Some spills don't leave a stain right away. They settle slowly. Like confusion after a rollout. Like distrust after a reorg. The change itself might be right, but the way it lands can turn progress into pushback. People nod in meetings, then retreat in practice. Not because they dislike the outcome, but because they weren't included in forming the path. The spill wasn't technical. It wasn't procedural. It was emotional. A mix of timing, tone, and top-down pressure that hardened resistance instead of clearing the space for trust.

The cleanup begins not with new tools or faster workflows. It begins with what the team is willing to retire. Habits. Documents. Defenses. Cleanup is unlearning. Project janitors know that culture shifts when people stop clinging to what once worked and start seeing the cost of keeping it. You clear the way, visibly. Confidently. You model the change before you ask for adoption. That is what breaks resistance, not force but influence. Not pressure but patience.

And when the cleanup sticks, it is not just because you stayed to enforce it. It is because you made room for the team to make it their own. Change holds when they own it. Not because it was perfect. Because it was shared. That is the goal of every cleanup, not control but transfer. A new rhythm, started by you, and sustained by them.

People don't resist change. They resist being changed.
-- Peter Senge

Adding the Polish

Change doesn't shine right away. Even when the cleanup works, even when the team begins to move, the new path still looks rough. Missteps happen. Old habits return. Some days feel like progress. Others feel like starting over. Some of that is just inherited impulse, reflexes from the old way. Time and repetition lock it down. The polish comes later. After the dust settles. After the rhythm holds. The project janitor doesn't declare victory too early. They stay long enough to reinforce what works, to sand down the sharp edges, and to make sure the change endures.

Polish is not decoration. It's reinforcement. You repeat the walkthroughs. You revisit the work. Observe it. Monitor it. Watch for the cues that show the change is holding. You check that the spill hasn't crept back under a new name. When it does, mop it. Just because the team is on a call doesn't mean they're locked into the discussion. The project janitor doesn't assume the new process will hold on its own. They confirm it. Quietly. Consistently. Not by hovering, but by being present. Available. A steady hand nearby until the team no longer needs it. A steady tune until they sing on their own.

Janitor's Keyring

Change that lasts isn't imposed, it's practiced. The project janitor clears the clutter, sets the rhythm, and stays just long enough to let the new habits take root. Because when the team carries the tune, the cleanup is complete.

The Wisdom Within: The Pied Piper and the Cats

There was once a village overrun with cats. They weren't wild or vicious. Just everywhere. On rooftops and rafters. In storerooms, under desks, curled in cabinets. They overturned inkpots, scattered ledgers, purred through council meetings, and slept soundly through every call to marshal them away. The townspeople had long given up trying to herd them. No plan lasted. No rule stuck. The more they tried to shoo or shout, the more the cats spread. What began as a few kittens had become a full infestation with no resolution. Cats.

Then one morning, a stranger arrived. He wore no badge. Made no lofty claims. He simply nodded once at the mayor, then raised a fife to his lips. The sound was strange, soft, winding, childlike in its simplicity. But it carried. Not as a command, but as an invitation. One by one, the cats lifted their heads. Ears twitched. Eyes narrowed. Paws stirred. And slowly, they followed.

Through alleyways and courtyards. Past the archive shed, the old proclamation board, the long-forgotten meeting tent. No traps. No pressure. Only the tune, gently repeating. Familiar enough to follow. Curious enough to trust.

The stranger walked to the edge of town. Then into the fields. Then to a hill. And as he climbed, the cats followed. Every single one. When he disappeared over the ridge, they disappeared with him.

The village fell silent. No more scratched floors. No toppled shelves. No hissing or lanterns clanking, knocked to the floor. For the first time in years, the mayor's chair sat clean. Furless. And when the townspeople looked for the stranger to thank him or pay him, they found he was already gone.

Some cats won't come when called. They walk their own path. You won't fix it by yelling louder. The cleanup begins not with orders, but with rhythm. With patience. With presence. The piper didn't chase, poke, pull, or drag. He just played. And the cats followed. Not because they were forced to, but because the tune gave them something better to follow than the mess they had made. That is the project janitor's task. Not to drive people out, but to walk slightly ahead, playing something worth walking toward. Play.

-- Brothers Grimm, as told by a Project Janitor

Adding to Your Toolbox

Acknowledge the resistance: Do not frame it as sabotage. Recognize it as a natural defense of the familiar, shaped by past disruptions and broken promises.

Sweep before you push: Clean up legacy stories, fears, and habits that stand in the way of new adoption. Listen for what lingers beneath the surface.

Spot the polish without substance: Identify when a process looks complete but lacks real usage or value. Surface the hollowness gently.

Hold up the mirror: Help the team see that what once worked may no longer fit. Show, don't shame.

Pilot change quietly: Roll out small, low-risk examples of the new way. Invite curiosity before demanding commitment.

Follow their rhythm: Make it easier to align than to resist. Reduce friction so that adoption feels natural, not forced.

Watch for signs of echo: Change sticks when teams repeat it on their own. Look for signs they are moving without your lead.

Reinforce without hovering: Be present enough to support, but not so close that you dominate. Let their comfort with the new grow.

Sweep clutter visibly: Model the cleanup. Clear unused tools, outdated reports, and meaningless steps to make room for what works.

Let go of control: Do not chase compliance. Create conditions where participation feels like the team's own decision.

Keep the tune alive: Stay long enough to ensure the rhythm holds. When the steps are theirs, step back.

Chapter 15
Polishing the Tarnish: Revealing the Treasure Hidden in Chaos

Executive Summary

This chapter explores the quiet work of recovery. Not reinvention, but recognition. Chaos is not the problem. It is the catalyst that brings the real problem to light. It reveals what was buried, not broken. The project janitor listens. They do not impose change. They uncover it. Beneath the mess, there is often something that still fits. A plan that once made sense. A purpose that still holds true.

Using the story of the Thames Tunnel and the fable of the pearl diver, this chapter shows how polishing the tarnish isn't about achieving perfection. It's about knowing when to stop scrubbing and start seeing. Project janitors do not chase clarity. They restore it. Because when the team sees the value for themselves and carries it forward, the shine returns. And what lasts isn't only the surface. It's the structure beneath.

The Mess at Hand

Chaos doesn't knock. It kicks the door in. Schedules scatter. Roles blur. The system of record floods with incidents. You're not sure who's running what anymore. Everyone's busy. And somehow, despite the motion, the standups, the endless pings, no one feels in control. But for the project janitor, this isn't new. It's not even a surprise. They've learned something others haven't. Chaos is the catalyst for change. Not a failure. A flare. A signal that something buried is trying to surface. Truth. Value. Priority. Purpose. The mess isn't just what's broken. It's announcing that something wants to be revealed.

Most teams try to silence the noise. Ignore it. Patch the leak. Reframe the update. But the project janitor listens instead. Because buried inside the static is a clue. A direction. The missed dependency no one logged. The lost data that no one questions. The workflow that loops instead of lands. Chaos does not invent these problems. It reveals them. It scrapes away the polish of presentation and lets the real issues speak. And if you are listening closely, you will hear what matters most. Not what was in the last slide deck. What is really driving fear, friction, or fatigue. That is how we begin to spot the tarnish.

Tarnish forms when something valuable is left exposed. Not ruined. Just dulled. That is what chaos reveals. The hidden cost of neglected clarity. The price of divergence. Every outdated workflow. Every fuzzy metric. Every team pretending alignment while quietly circling in confusion. Chaos does not cause that. It shows where the shine has faded. And once you see it, you cannot unsee it. That is the moment the project janitor steps in. Not to polish for appearance, but to recover what was once clean, once clear, once known. Chaos exposes the mess. And the path forward.

The Cleaning Strategy

Chaos does not arrive with answers. It arrives with mirrors. Reflections of what teams ignore under pressure, revealing what they truly value. What they fight to preserve, even when everything else slips, shows you what matters most. That's why the project janitor runs toward the clutter instead of fleeing from it. Not every mess is a malfunction. Some are echoes of truth. Misaligned expectations. Priorities that were never categorized. Commitments that held more weight than the charter admitted. Chaos is the catalyst for change, not because it disrupts plans, but because it reveals what was missing from them in the first place.

The value was never gone. It was just hidden. That is the lesson chaos teaches. Teams forget why they started. Sponsors forget what they asked for. Stakeholders raise new demands and call them baseline. But somewhere inside the noise, the original purpose is still there. Dull, maybe, but intact. The project janitor doesn't hunt for perfection. They look for what still holds. Not every layer of grout haze hides a cracked tile. Like a pearl in a shell that looks too plain to open, what matters most is often still inside, waiting to be brought into view.

Most recovery projects still have good materials. Solid ideas. People who care. What they lack is alignment. Somewhere along the way, the pieces stopped fitting. Meetings got louder than priorities. Metrics replaced momentum. Time clouded the target. And now it all feels stuck. But buffing doesn't add substance. It clears what's in the way. The project janitor does not rebuild from scratch. They step in with a cloth, some light, and patience to reveal what was already there. Unfinished, maybe, but true.

To listen beneath the noise, the project janitor begins quietly. With presence. They watch for chaos that keeps surfacing. Who interrupts whom. Which questions are asked but never answered. They map stakeholder priorities by what is repeated, not just what is written. They run reviews in the middle of the storm, not after it ends. They ask the team to name their concerns. They pull the thread on forgotten tasks, orphaned decisions, and effort that no longer connects to purpose. Because in chaos, it is easy to confuse motion with value. The project janitor slows the pace just enough to see what is really moving, and in which direction it moves.

The cleaning strategy is this: you don't search for a new shell. You open the one they tossed aside. You don't fix chaos by layering more process. You clear just enough to see what was always there. The project janitor begins with what still holds. Plans that once made sense. Agreements that meant something. Goals that still ring true. Then they bring those lines forward and sweep away what no longer fits. This is not reinvention. It is recovery. It is the decision to look again before walking away. Because like a pearl in an oyster that seemed too plain to matter, the value was never missing. It was waiting to be seen.

Scrub Away the Chaos

To scrub away chaos, you do not start by scrubbing. You start by sweeping the floor. You inspect what was swept. You put away those useful things that fell long ago. Then, you scrub.

Sweeping the floor: In a chaotic project, everyone's moving fast but often, no one's moving forward. Conversations loop. Dashboards mislead. Urgency drowns intention. The project janitor slows the rhythm without saying so. They shorten the updates. Clear blocked queues. Prioritize the emergencies. Instead of chasing every problem, they reduce the motion.

Inspect what was swept: Once the pace slows, the haze dissolves. Still, not everything worth saving will announce itself. Some of it remains half-buried. A long-ignored test script that still flags the right failure in every release. A load-bearing beam marked for removal that still passes every inspection. A discontinued lab procedure that delivered more consistent control results than the current one. The project janitor does not reframe the work. They reopen it. They ask what still fits. What still belongs. What was never broken, just buried. What could shine. When teams name these pieces for themselves, the cleanup begins to hold. Because they are not being pushed. They are remembering.

Put away the useful: You do not shape the project around what failed. You shape it around what still glints under the grime. One element, recovered and re-centered, can carry more weight than a full rewrite. A schedule that still fits. A client outcome that still matters. A working relationship that still stands. That is the anchor. Not the noise, not the damage, not the sprint metrics. The project janitor lets that single glimmer guide the reset. They wipe just far enough for the team to see what might shine again.

That is how order returns, not because everything is new, but because something true has regained its luster. Let that clarity hold the weight before you move again. Now scrub.

Lessons from the Janitor's Closet

London, 1825: The Thames Tunnel was meant to be simple. A passage beneath the river to spare Londoners the tides, the ferries, the wait. No grandeur. No symbolism. Simply a clean solution to a real problem, a way to connect the city. For a time, it looked promising. The plans were drawn. The shield was ready. The dig began. But almost immediately, chaos fogged the landscape. Even in the early days, the ground whispered that this project would not go as planned.

The soil was softer than expected. The river above pressed harder than the engineers had prepared for. The experimental tunneling shield, though innovative, creaked under the pressure. Leaks emerged like the river was angry with the belief it could be tamed. Mud seeped through seams. Crews worked by candlelight in air so stale it choked their breath. Each foot forward came with collapse. What started with the anticipation of an engineering feat now felt more like an undoing than a breakthrough.

The project stalled. Then stopped. Investors lost faith. Headlines blamed mismanagement. Workers quit. Others refused to go back underground to work. The tunnel flooded again, then again. Each effort to regain control revealed how little there had ever been. No one trusted the tunneling shield. Or the schedule. Or each other. Leadership stopped leading. The plan sat untouched. Decisions drifted. And those still showing up each day did what people do when no one's steering. They stayed busy. But nothing got done. No one was searching for pearls.

The first sign of recovery came as a question. Someone asked why the plans had stopped. Another pulled the last working drawing from a drawer and flattened it on the table. The paper was dusty and wrinkled, a blueprint for a structure never built. The ink had bled. But the path was still there. That's how the project janitor arrives. Not with answers, but with purpose. They study what's been left behind. They ask what still makes sense. They listen for the part of the project that hasn't quit. Because underneath the collapse, something always remains. Something worth brushing off and holding up to the light.

The project janitor does not redraw the plans. They clear the table. They wipe the dust. They tape the edges of the old schematic so it lies flat again. Steady. They mark the sections that still hold true and cross out the ones that missed the mark. Then they bring the team in to question it. Not to debate them. To involve them. Because clarity is not handed down by mandate. It's uncovered together. That's how forgotten paths return. Not through force, but by collaboration. Patience. By walking the line again, inch by inch, until the shape beneath the collapse starts to feel real. Truly possible. Solid.

They did not call it a relaunch. No ribbon-cutting. No speeches. One day, someone walked back into the tunnel. This time with better bracing. Better light. Fewer assumptions. The shield was inspected, strengthened, and set again. Progress returned slowly, not as a celebration, but as a rhythm. Tasks that had once scattered found order. People started asking questions out loud. Teams met without scripts. And for the first time in a long while, each step had purpose.

The Thames Tunnel eventually opened, of course. It spanned the riverbed, just as the original plans had promised. But the value wasn't only in what connected two shores. It was in what reconnected the team. The pearl wasn't the tunnel. It was what the tunnel had restored. Patience. Alignment. Shared momentum. Trust. The ability to move forward without collapsing. The project janitor didn't build the shield. They helped others see it could still do the job. That was the quiet work. Not fixing the failure. Revealing the part that was always strong enough to last. It has. Because chaos didn't break the tunnel. Tarnish removed, the chaos revealed what wasn't properly planned in the first place.

Spills and Cleanup

Tarnish doesn't arrive as failure. It arrives as neglect. Polish forgotten. When chaos hits and teams scramble, most are too busy moving to notice what's fading. A goal unspoken. A process unexamined. A decision forced out of sequence, then rationalized. And the longer the smudges are ignored, the more they harden. Not into rot, but into routine. That's the real spill: when misalignment becomes habit, and the team stops asking why everything feels directionless. Because when motion replaces meaning, the shine fades. Not all at once. It dulls quietly. Until no one remembers what it used to look like clean.

In the scramble to reclaim order, teams often polish the wrong things. They stage meetings, publish dashboards, and reorganize roles. Not to restore alignment, but to simulate it. With busy work. Energy replaces clarity. Everything looks better. But the problems remain. Underneath the metrics, the same missteps repeat. Decisions still sit. Priorities still blur. A shiny status report means nothing if no one believes in the goal. That is the danger of fast cleanup. It masks the mess instead of clearing it. Listen to the chaos.

Project janitors do not rush to restore appearances. They return to what remains. A working agreement still respected. A goal that still stirs conviction. A piece of code, a value map, or a sketch on the white board that still makes sense. They ask what still fits. What was solid before the noise. Then they clear the buildup around it. The assumptions. The distractions. The misguided efforts to polish something broken. Because real cleanup is not reinvention. It is recovery. We do not fix chaos. We reveal what still works beneath it.

We do this work to restore more than progress. We restore belief. In the goal. In the team. In the idea that forward is still possible. The treasure is not a deliverable. It is trust. It is the moment a worn-out team sees something clear again and knows it matters. Project janitors do not invent that clarity. They reveal it. They help others see what never stopped being true. Polish is not decoration. It is confirmation that what remains is still worth seeing. Remove the tarnish.

A first-hand account from Isambard Kingdom Brunel, who was deeply involved in the Thames Tunnel project:

I was at that moment giving directions to the three men, in what manner they ought to proceed in the dark, to effect their escape, when they and I were knocked down and covered by a part of the timber stage. I struggled under water for some time, and at length extricated myself from the stage; and by swimming and being forced by the water, I gained the eastern arch, where I got a better footing, and was enabled, by laying hold of the railway rope, to pause a little in the hope of encouraging the men who had been knocked down at the same time with myself.
-- Isambard Kingdom Brunel, letter to the directors, 1828

Adding the Polish

Polishing is not graceful. It's not about a finish line. It comes after the mess has been sorted and something solid remains. Like a pearl pulled from a rough shell, the shine doesn't come easily. You buff it. Slowly. Carefully. You check. You go over it again. The cloth works harder than it seems. But your hands don't mind. Because you're not just working. You're holding something worth the effort. You're holding something real. That's what polish means. Quiet care. Earned clarity.

You don't point at the shine. You let others notice it. A clean path speaks for itself. One person sees the order return and begins to trust it. Another checks a detail and finds it right. No announcement. No push. Simply quiet agreement that something here works again. That's what polish does. It gives the team a reason to believe in the work without being convinced. What lasts is like a precious stone. It doesn't fade. It holds its shape quietly. It withstands the pressure and shines anyway.

Polish is where the last illusions fall away. You see the uneven cut, the seam that never fit, the part that looked fine under dust but doesn't align in daylight. That's why the cloth moves slowly. Because the perfect shine is never fully realized. This is the moment you confirm the work. Not the effort. The alignment. That what you've recovered still fits. That the plan connects. That the team understands the purpose and can carry it without you. Polish is not just shine. It is the confirmation that the pieces hold together. That the structure is sound. That forward is not just possible. It is inevitable.

Janitor's Keyring

Clarity that endures isn't invented. It's revealed. The project janitor doesn't rush the cleanup or reframe the work. They slow the motion, study the mess, and recover what still fits. Because when the team sees the value for themselves and carries it forward, the tarnish fades. The treasure remains. And the work lasts.

The Wisdom Within: The Pearl Inside the Shell

There was once a pearl diver who worked the quiet coves beyond the rocks, where the water ran deep and the shells lay buried in layers of sand. Each morning before the sun touched the bay, the diver rowed out alone and dropped beneath the waves, searching the ocean floor for what might be hidden there.

At first, every shell was treated with care. The diver opened each one, slowly and patiently, washing away grit, prying gently to see what might lie inside. Most were empty. Some were shattered. Others held nothing but salt and silt. But once in a while, there was something else. A pearl. Dull at first, small and stubborn, but unmistakable.

The diver kept going.

But as the seasons passed, the work grew harder. The sea grew colder. The shells all looked the same. And the pearls, if any, were harder to find. So, the diver began to sort faster. Open less. Judge sooner. Every shell that looked too ordinary, too plain, was tossed aside unopened. There was no time for what did not sparkle.

One day, after a long dive with little to show, the diver sat on the shore beside a mound of discarded shells. On a whim, they cracked one open. Not one they had picked that day, but one they had thrown away. A rough one. A small one. A plain, battered shell.

Inside was a pearl. Not perfect. Not polished. But there, resting quietly all along.

That is the work. You do not sort by shine. You search with patience. In recovery, it is easy to skip what looks too rough to keep. Ideas that went quiet. Agreements that frayed. Deliverables half-formed and left behind. But polish is not about making something new. It is about seeing what was missed. It is about trusting that under the mess, something of value still remains.

Not every shell holds a pearl. But some do. And when you find one, the shape of the whole project begins to change. Because now the team is not chasing sparkle. They are holding something real. That is what it means to polish the tarnish. To reveal the treasure hidden in chaos. To believe that what endures is worth the effort. And to slow down long enough to see it.

See it.

-- Project Janitor

Adding to Your Toolbox

Step toward the noise: Chaos is not the enemy. It is the signal. Approach it with presence, not panic. Listen before you act.

Spot what keeps surfacing: Watch for the repeated friction points. Questions left unanswered. Priorities that outlast plans. These reveal what matters most.

Slow the rhythm: Pause the flurry of motion long enough to separate noise from signal. Clarity cannot surface if the pace stays frantic.

Reopen what was tossed aside: Look again at the abandoned plans, the quiet deliverables, the tools no longer mentioned. Some still fit.

Find what still holds: Before creating something new, find what is already solid. A goal, an agreement, a method that still works.

Clear the buildup: Remove distractions, assumptions, and procedural clutter that have dulled the work. Strip down to what connects.

Recenter on purpose: Let the work refocus around the part that still matters. Not everything, just the part that shines through.

Anchor progress to what is real: Shape recovery around what the team rediscovers together. Let shared recognition guide the next step.

Reveal, don't reframe: Do not repackage the work to look clean. Help the team see what was always valuable. Let them carry it forward.

Chapter 16
Ready for Inspection: Testing, Training, and Transition

Executive Summary

This chapter examines the later phases of a project, where calm progress often conceals untested assumptions. Although checklists are complete and status reports appear positive, true readiness is often unproven. The chapter emphasizes that projects are judged not by what was planned but by what is handed over and how it performs under pressure.

The chapter draws a clear contrast between projects that appeared ready and those that actually were. One skipped testing and failed under stress. Another delivered a functioning system but never trained users, leading to failure in operation. Only the third succeeded, because the team tested thoroughly, trained consistently, and transitioned with care.

Through the real-world lens of the Y2K global remediation effort the chapter shows how systems fail not from sabotage, but from omission. One skipped test. One missed lesson. One unsteady handoff. The project janitor doesn't wait to find out if the work holds. They confirm it does, before the wind arrives.

The Mess at Hand

Some projects reach their final phase with quiet momentum rather than urgency. Tasks are marked complete. Reports show progress. The schedule remains on track. Satisfying boredom. But beneath that calm is something more fragile: the assumption of readiness. Testing is penciled in but often unproven. Training is outlined but often incomplete.

Transition is near but not fully prepared. Nothing is visibly wrong. Yet everything depends on what happens next. Years of work stand to be judged. And that is when the project janitor pivots. Not for closure. Not yet for lessons learned. But to make sure the deliverables stand up when they must.

The danger in late-stage projects isn't disruption. It's assumption. A checklist can show a sea of green indicators yet be unconfirmed. A walkthrough can look smooth without pressure applied, without looking behind the curtain. Readiness is not the checkbox beside each milestone. It is a condition that must be earned through diligence. A state that must be proven. And proof takes friction. Tests that fail before they pass. Inspections that raise eyebrows. Questions that uncover what process has not been trained. Simulations that feel unnecessary until they are needed most. These aren't extras. They are the work. Because when the transition begins, there is no time to wonder if the team is ready. They either are, or they aren't. That's the mess at hand.

Projects are rarely judged by what was promised, but by what is handed over. They are judged when someone new turns the key, clicks the icon, opens the door. The first impression becomes the lasting one. And if that moment fails, it won't matter how well the project was planned. The project janitor understands this. That readiness is not a headline. It is a handoff. It lives in the smallest places. Labels that make sense. Guides that get used. Systems that perform under load. The job now is to prove that it works, not to hope it does.

The Cleaning Strategy

This is where the final work begins. The project has already been recovered. The project janitor held firm on scope, rebuild the schedule, tracked, and met it. The mess is cleaned. What remains is no longer about catching up. It's about proving readiness for handoff. Testing what was built. Training those who will carry it. Planning the moment the keys, and the broom, are passed. The project janitor shifts from stabilizer to steward. Not assuming the structure will hold but confirming it. Walking it. Watching. Handing someone else the bucket and seeing if the water runs. Does the team know what to do next?

Some builds stand on first use. Others don't. And it rarely comes down to the blueprint. It comes down to what was tested, what was shared, and whether anyone else knew how to step in when it mattered. Some teams pour the slab, rush the cure, and call it done. Some walk through once, blink, and assume the frame will stand. But others take a different path. They pause. They test. They teach. They let someone else try the latch, follow the instructions, reset the breaker, cycle the system. Not because they expect failure, but because they want to see what is missing while there is still time to fix it.

The difference never shows on paper. A project can check every box and still come apart. Testing, training, and transition can all appear complete. They can meet the spec. They can pass review. But only when pressure comes do we see what is truly ready. The shortcuts don't fail in the handoff meeting. They fail in use. Under heat, strain, turnover, scale. The moment someone expects it to work, and it doesn't. That's when we learn whether the effort was built to last or just built to finish. And the project janitor doesn't wait for that moment. They simulate it. Invite it. Because when the handoff comes, they don't want surprise. They want confirmation.

There were once three projects. The first project looked finished. Walls stood. Fixtures hung. The schedule remained stable. The punch list came back clean. But no one tested the ground beneath. The team skipped soil surveys. They left the back wall without insulation. They poured footings without rebar. They ran undersized wiring that could not carry the expected load. They sealed and buried plumbing lines without pressure-testing any of them. From the outside, everything looked complete. But when the inspectors came to stress the systems, they flexed and failed. Failover never kicked in. There weren't any. The team passed the drawings. They met the deadlines. But they never tested where it mattered. Test.

The second project looked stable. The systems ran sound and tested clean. Interfaces worked. Reports loaded. The workflows matched the business cases. But no one showed the users how to operate them. The team scheduled training sessions, but between the scramble of delivery and the logistics of pulling everyone to campus, they never happened. They wrote manuals but never walked through them. A few team members poked around, made guesses, and moved on. Then the turnover began. The first critical handoff collapsed. The help desk lit up. One missed keystroke corrupted a file. A default setting stalled billing. Ultimately, the system delivered what was built. But the rollout failed because no one trained the people meant to carry it. Train.

The third project did not launch with a celebration. It launched with a checklist. The team tested every path, not just the happy ones. They let things fail early, fixed them, and failed them again. They brought in the future owners, walked them through real use cases, and asked them to try. Not watch. Try. They fixed what confused them. They labeled what mattered. They handed off early, then stepped back and watched. When the pressure huffed and puffed, nothing collapsed. When the go-live date came, it was not quiet just because nothing happened. It was quiet because everything had already happened. The handoff was not an event. It was the result of preparation. Test. Train. Transition.

Scrub Away the Chaos

Most late-phase projects look ready on paper. That is the danger. Green dashboards, signed specs, and polite silence in meetings do not confirm readiness. The project janitor scrubs deeper. They reframe status updates into testable, measurable outcomes. They ask what has been tried, not just what has been built. They spot risk in the gaps between teams, where assumptions go unchallenged. Readiness features on the report, but it proves itself through trials, load tests. The project janitor introduces action early and often, through simulation, sprint reviews, walkthroughs, early handoffs, and quiet fire drills that expose what looks complete but is not.

Training isn't a slide deck. Transition isn't a calendar date. The project janitor knows that both will fail if they're treated like tasks instead of dynamic processes. They scrub every dependency for continuity. They monitor sequencing and priority to ensure deliverables land in the right order. They build readiness into the rhythm of delivery, not as an afterthought. Training happens peer-to-peer, over time, by doing. Transition begins when the end users first interact with the work, not when the project closes. What holds up isn't what's handed off. It's what has already been carried. That's the test of a real handoff. And it doesn't happen unless someone stays to scrub away assumptions and confirm what sticks.

Lessons from the Janitor's Closet

Y2K was the deadline the world didn't miss. Not because the threat was overblown, but because the cleanup came first. For years, engineers, analysts, and architects combed through decades of code and hardware to prepare for a date that couldn't be moved: 1/1/00. They weren't chasing attention. They were chasing certainty. And when midnight struck, the lights stayed on. Planes flew. Banks settled. Engineers slept. Because the mess had already been scrubbed. Quietly. Thoroughly. Without spectacle. It made headlines for what didn't crash. But what didn't crash was the point. Nothing failed because the preparations delivered.

Most people remember the jokes. The canned food. The basement generators. The anxious glances at digital clocks. Late, late nights. This project janitor remembers it all. What we sometimes forget, though, is how much got done. Governments and corporations didn't just patch a bug. They inventoried every legacy system, interviewed every vendor, mapped dependencies that had never been documented, and funded years of groundwork. What began as a two-digit date became a test of global coordination. This wasn't hype. It was a rehearsal. The largest one modern history had ever seen.

The testing came first. Not once, but repeatedly. Banks ran rollover simulations. Airports scheduled mock transitions. IT teams cloned environments, set clocks ahead, and watched what failed. If a system buckled, it buckled early. That was the point. Every test was a rehearsal. Every rehearsal was a cleanup. This was not the kind of testing that fit in a sprint or wrapped up in a single cycle. It was layered. It was stubborn. It was built to break things before those things broke the world. And for every environment that passed without a hitch, there were hundreds that didn't - until they did.

Training mattered just as much as testing. Teams outlined plans for what to do if the lights flickered, if the clocks reset, if the systems stalled. Operators reviewed the steps. Leads documented contingencies. Executives walked through their response protocols. Entire teams stayed overnight, not because they expected failure, but because they refused to allow it. They practiced for every possible outcome. Even the public received guidance through news segments, bank statements, and mailed notices that explained what might happen. When midnight neared, people did not wait in fear. They stood ready. Because someone had already shown them what to do and how to do it, no matter what came.

Transition didn't arrive as a moment. It arrived as continuity. Systems stayed online because someone had already watched them fail in test runs. And fixed them. Operators knew what to do because they had walked through the drill. Even midnight didn't feel like a deadline. It felt like a checkpoint. One more log entry in a night full of them. That's the mark of a real transition. When the instant doesn't wobble. When the weight passes cleanly from those who built it to those who must now carry it.

Some project janitors didn't go home after midnight. They stayed a few hours longer. Not because they expected failure, but because they wanted to see it through. To watch the system breathe. To hear the click of the next shift logging in. To feel the quiet hold. It was a silent celebration. The kind no dashboard captures. The moment when preparation becomes trust. Not in the tools, but in the handoff. We did the work. And in the end, that is what the project janitor leaves behind. Not just stability. Silent stewardship.

That's the paradox. The better the work, the less it calls attention to itself. *Success hides the evidence of its own necessity.*

True readiness leaves no trophy. No launch event. No viral photo. It lives in the systems that hold, the teams that carry on, and the clients who never notice the moment everything could have gone wrong. That is the legacy of the project janitor. They do not just deliver. They prepare others to learn, to take ownership, to endure. And that quiet continuity, the kind that survives handoff and pressure, is not the absence of failure. It is the presence of readiness. Be ready.

Spills and Cleanup

Y2K is often remembered as a non-event. That's the myth. The cleanup happened before it became one. Engineers at companies like Hewlett-Packard started in 1996, years before the deadline. This project janitor was there as a witness. The teams combed through legacy systems, rewrote code, validated interfaces, and ran scenario after scenario. It wasn't exciting work. It wasn't glamorous. But it mattered. The spill wasn't technical. It was historical. Because when success looks like nothing happened, sometimes the truth gets lost.

No planes fell. No power grids shut down. No global markets collapsed. And because none of that happened, some believed the risk had been exaggerated. But that's the mistake. That's the spill. To discount what you don't see. The cleanup wasn't dramatic. It was measured. Planned. The systems remained stable because someone checked. Rechecked. Stayed late. Readiness passed inspection because someone prepared it to do so.

At Hewlett-Packard alone, thousands of engineers contributed. They mapped dependencies, tested systems, simulated failure, and rehearsed recovery. That's what a project janitor does. They don't wait for the mess. They prevent it. Y2K wasn't a false alarm. It was the best possible outcome. A global test of discipline, collaboration, and technical stewardship. And it held.

The final spill is cultural. When work is invisible, its value can be overlooked. Project janitors accept that. They know the job is not to be noticed. It's to be trusted. But even so, history should remember that many stayed late. Someone ran the last test. Someone made sure the handoff would last. That's what kept the lights on.

The reward of a thing well done is having done it.
-- Ralph Waldo Emerson

Adding the Polish

Some structures fall before they're used. Others stand for generations. The difference isn't always what was drawn. It's what was proven. Tested. Shared. Handed off with care. That is what real readiness looks like. Not the end of the project, but the moment it must bear weight.

The polish comes later, but it is earned early. In the simulations that fail before they pass. In the walkthroughs that slow down to show someone new what to do next. In the training that doesn't come from slides, but from watching someone else reset the breaker and asking why. That's how a handoff becomes real.

In the story of three projects shared in the cleaning strategy, testing, training, and transition can all appear complete. Still, the results depend on the project janitor. One followed the blueprint but left before it was tested. Another developed and tested the system but never trained the team. A third stood beside the work until the others could carry it. What stood wasn't just the frame. It was the preparation, the tests, the time, the quiet training that stayed behind. Transition couldn't be blown down. Real readiness wasn't a ribbon-cutting. It was a door opened by someone new.

That's what the title means: Ready for Inspection. Not ready in theory. Ready in practice. The project janitor doesn't wait for the moment of inspection. They prepare for it. They welcome it. They don't fear the pressure. They invite it. Because when the structure stands, when the lights stay on, when the next team takes over without pause, that's not luck. That's the polish.

Janitor's Keyring

Readiness must be secured through testing, training, and transition. The project janitor introduces real conditions early, so failure shows up before the real work begins. They don't assume a smooth handoff; they prove it.

The Wisdom Within: The Three Bracing Builders

Long ago, three builders were each given the same charge: to raise shelter before the season turned. The wind had already begun to change. The deadline was fixed. The storm would not wait, and neither would the inspection it carried.

The first builder worked fast. He raised his frame in days, measured nothing, tested nothing, and left no trace of how the work had been done. "It stands," he said. And the wind was on the horizon.

The second builder built stronger. He used better timber and sealed the joints. Tested well. He trained no one. "It's all there," he said.

"They'll figure it out." Would they? No one knew how to close and secure the shutters. And the wind was on the horizon.

The third builder moved with care. They tested each joint before building the next. They trained the ones who would inherit the work. And before stepping away, they walked the final circle, doors latched, seals checked, nothing left incomplete. The transition had already begun. And the wind was on the horizon.

Then the storm arrived. Not a fable's huff, but the true breath of change: pressure, use, time. It pushed on all three buildings. The first one fell, untested. The second one failed, untrained. The third one stood. Not untouched. But stable.

Inspection isn't the enemy. It's when the truth arrives. If you've tested, trained, and handed things off with care, there's nothing to fear. The wind is always on the horizon.

-- Adapted from *The Three Little Pigs*, as told by a Project Janitor

Adding to Your Toolbox

Add real conditions early: Testing is not a checkbox. Simulate real use cases before launch so failure shows up while there is still time to fix it.

Prove what's been built: Validate each deliverable not by report but by use. Confirm workflows, settings, and labels make sense to others, not just the builders.

Train in practice, not theory: Build confidence through repetition. Training must happen before the transition begins, not after it fails.

Let others test the system: Invite future owners to click through, configure, reset, and recover. Watch what confuses them. Fix it.

Confirm continuity: Check for sequencing gaps, missed handoffs, and unclear ownership. If the rhythm stutters, the system is not yet ready.

Quietly rehearse the handoff: Let the new team try without you. Observe what holds. Adjust what slips. Readiness is earned, not declared.

Stay for the shift: Readiness ends with presence. Remain long enough to see the next team take over and the system hold without help.

Chapter 17
The Point of the Cleanup: Closing the Project with Confidence

Executive Summary

Projects don't end when the work stops. They end when the work stands. Closure isn't decoration. It's discipline. It's the inbox that stays quiet. The sequence that continues without prompting. The decision that no longer needs defense. In this chapter, we explore the final act of stewardship, how project janitors prepare to leave from the start, and how they make their absence the point.

We'll look at what happens when closure is skipped, and how unfinished work creates lasting problems. We'll also show what it takes to finish a project in a way that lets others move forward without confusion. Some projects end quietly. Others resurface through support tickets, missed deadlines, and repeated confusion. But when the final steps are handled with care, the product of the project stands on its own and others can follow it with confidence.

That's the work. That's the arrival. That's the point of the cleanup. That's the project janitor's definition of closure.

The Mess at Hand

The project looks complete. The team deployed the code. The roof passed inspection. The ceremony ended. Leadership reassigned people to the next priority. Still, the project isn't closed. Not really. No one submitted the final milestone documents. The client didn't sign the maintenance and operations plan. No one sent the final invoices. No one briefed the help desk. The tracker still shows unresolved dependencies, just hidden deeper now. The work sits paused behind a polished surface. The final handoffs remain unclear. No one scheduled a final review. The permits still need signatures. No one issued the acceptance certificates. It's a mess. Everyone assumes the work is done because no one checks closely enough to confirm the final steps. And that is the risk: closure assumed, not delivered.

Closure isn't just forgotten. It's often abandoned. Time rarely allows full attention once the punch list becomes someone else's problem. So a few questions come in. A support ticket. A billing dispute. A missing archive request. Weeks pass before anyone realizes the escalation path was never finalized, or that production support can't access the repository. Tasks reopen one by one, but no one owns them anymore. The cleanup begins to tarnish. What looked like a closed project becomes a string of steady callbacks, reopened tickets, and emails from irate clients. And every one of them costs more to mop than it would have, had someone stayed to close things right the first time.

By the end of a project, even the most disciplined teams feel the weight. Fatigue sets in. The energy moves to the next initiative, and attention follows it out the door. People vanish. Meetings shrink. The inbox quiets. Velocity drops. The last mile becomes the most vulnerable. Not because it is the hardest, but because no one stays to walk it. The final documents go untouched. The lessons learned session gets postponed, then quietly forgotten. What mattered for months now doesn't even make the monthly status report. We celebrate too early. We leave too soon. And the work, though mostly finished, is never fully closed. It's left to float in space.

The Cleaning Strategy

One of the drawbacks of defining a project as finite is that leadership sometimes calls it finished before it's truly over. Budgets veer. Charts flatten. Someone declares victory and reallocates the team. Project leaders get reassigned mid-close, or worse, removed entirely. And what's left behind isn't a clean finish. It's scuffed. That's why the definition of done matters. Not just for scope, but for ownership. For timing. For accountability. A lingering project isn't closed simply because the shiny new contract arrives. It's often left behind because people have grown tired of it. They want to move on to something fresh. But closure isn't about novelty. It's about follow-through. A project is only closed when the work is verified, transitioned, secured, and accepted. Anything less is a closure adrift.

By the time most projects reach the finish line, the original project leader is already gone. Reassigned. Rotated out. Promoted. Or pushed aside. What remains is often not leadership. But someone has to carry the work forward. Not always a project manager by title. Sometimes it is a coordinator. Sometimes a contractor. Sometimes an admin who just knows where the paperwork is buried. In IT, it is often the person who will have the pleasure of supporting the system long after go-live. In construction, it is usually customer service. Not chosen, but present. Still at the desk with the service screen open, even if the lead has already moved on to the next site. They step up because someone must. They do not claim the title. But they carry the mop.

So, we welcome the next project janitor. They finish what others left behind. They review the final deliverables, match them to what was promised, and follow the trail until every box is checked. They confirm the operations plan was signed, the user guide was distributed, and someone knows how to run the monthly job. They schedule check-ins throughout the stabilization period, even when no one shows. They request the client sign off, even when it takes three reminders. Often more. They clear the inbox, close the tickets, archive the files, and turn out the lights. Quiet work. But the kind that keeps the next person from stepping into confusion.

Every project janitor needs a closing kit. It starts with a mental checklist built from experience. Has the client acknowledged receipt of what was delivered? Has support confirmed the handoff? Are the documents versioned, stored, and shared with the right people? Has every final payment been confirmed? Has access been withdrawn where it should be? The project janitor runs through these questions without ceremony. Not because they're glamorous, but because they're necessary. Closure is important. It's proof that the work was truly finished. No threads left dangling. No one left guessing.

It takes discipline to finish well. By the end, recognition fades. The spotlight beams elsewhere. Most people step away once the visible work is done. But the project janitor stays. They document the lessons learned. Hold the session with the team. File the results for the next project. Not to impress anyone, but to make sure the lessons stand. Now and in the future. They check what others left behind, confirm what still needs to happen, and walk through the final steps. They do it to finish the job right and to make sure no one else has to clean it up later.

Projects that close well don't just protect their own outcomes. They protect the ones that follow. When closure is clean, the next team doesn't waste hours hunting for documents, asking what went wrong, or guessing what was delivered. The team archives the signed acceptance form. They publish the final project report. They hand off the warranty documents, punch list, and maintenance schedule. They deliver as-built drawings and mark them final. They close the project contract or confirm the transition to ongoing terms. The support team starts from a stable handoff. Leadership sees real results, not just optimistic dashboards. And the client remembers the project for how well it ended, not how long it dragged on.

Closure is more than a phase. It's a mindset. It's the discipline to stay when others walk away. The project janitor doesn't just clean the site. They secure the result. They know that what gets left behind becomes someone else's starting point. So they finish it right. They complete the arc. To land with nothing left open.

The point of the cleanup - is to arrive. So, arrive.

That's the strategy. That's closure.

Scrub Away the Chaos

Although some efforts do not begin at the beginning, closure does. It takes shape before the team drafts a press release, before the kickoff deck takes form, before leadership assigns the first resources. Closure begins with early alignment. In the moment the concept takes shape. In the stir before the charter.

Still, by the time the project janitor joins the team, closure is no longer assured. Like the bearer who studies the map before lifting the lantern, the project janitor traces the intended path, even when the trail ahead is unclear. They do not wait for the way to be lit. They prepare to light it. Not with spectacle. With quiet certainty. Closure happens only when the destination is known, the path understood, and the work ready to be carried out, and followed through.

Project janitors steer the work already in motion. They do not alter the past, but they adjust what lies ahead. They clear what has grown over. They correct what slipped and make sure it stays aligned. They reset the markers so the project can reach its intended end. That may mean revisiting scope, extending timelines, or rebalancing resources, whatever makes closure possible. They do not always redraw the map. Instead, they make the final stretch walkable again. Quietly. Precisely. By restoring the path, not rerouting it.

Some projects diverge from the intended target. Not because the work breaks down, but because no one aims for closure. No one defines the landing. No one clarifies what it means to finish. The team focuses on delivery without direction, mistaking movement for momentum. Planning for closure may not guarantee a perfect end, but no project finishes well without a target. You cannot recover a path you never charted. You cannot correct a course you never chose. Closure begins when someone, anyone, decides that the ending matters. Quietly. Cleanly. Completely. That is not magic. That is discipline. That is the difference between done and closed.

Lessons from the Janitor's Closet

It began with design. In the charts, the calculations, the calibrated margins. Engineers never built it to return home. Its destination was the unknown. They built it to let go. They knew they would never chase it. Never rework it. Never retrieve it. So, they aligned everything: course, payload, protocols. Its target was assured long before the turn of a single screw. Voyager launched with confidence in the preparation. That is what real closure looks like. Not a shutdown. A release. Built to last.

And Voyager? The greatest lantern ever carried.

Voyager didn't wander a path to success any more than it wandered into existence. It arrived because every decision traced back to purpose. The team calibrated the systems for endless distance and tuned for burn sufficient to ensure separation from Earth's pull. They carefully timed each signal, ensuring clarity long after they themselves would be gone. They designed every transmission path to endure. Even the golden record, tucked like a message in a bottle spoke from intention. A way to say: we were here, and we finished what we started.

Projects that close well carry the same hallmark. You don't design them for return. You design them to stand on their own. To separate cleanly. To keep flying long after the team has disbanded. That means choosing tools that last, processes that endure, and transition paths that don't rely on someone remembering how things used to work. It means thinking ahead to the support team, the client, the one person left behind who didn't attend the demos. Closure means you thought of them. You targeted the handoff. You wrote the solution into the flight plan. As early as possible.

Voyager still flies. Beyond the planets. Beyond our grasp. It carries a message no one may ever hear, but it flies. Not because anyone still checks in, but because the team closed it right. That's not luck. That's legacy. Voyager did not loop back for a second chance. It did not pivot midstream or wait for approval. It flew. Straight. Stable. Ready. The engineers conceived it that way. They designed it. They built it. They tested it. They launched it with intention. It wasn't designed to reach a specific target. It was designed to leave. To hold course long after we lost signal. And that's closure, not destination, but direction. Not control, but release.

PLAYBOOK FOR PROJECT JANITORS

The project janitor chooses to lead toward the same legacy. Leave something that flies on its own. A system that runs. A platform that endures. A message that carries. Not because someone keeps watching, but because the work stands. Closure does not happen by accident. Begin to close from your first day on the project.

Spills and Cleanup

Milton B. Flashover was never elected. But you wouldn't know that by the way he entered a room. He walked with the posture of power, chin lifted just high enough to seem presidential, voice tuned for press clips, smile measured and constant. Appointed as Assistant Director of Statewide IT Administration, Milton held a title that sounded influential and a seat that should have been. His office oversaw technology for every cabinet-level agency across the state: health, education, labor, public safety. But while the scope was broad, his engagement was shallow. For two decades, he attended meetings, made appearances, dropped names. He built an image, not a legacy.

His signature move was the tie. Yes, the bright, gaudy, flashy necktie. Before every meeting, he would vanish into his office and reemerge with a new one: bold stripes, loud prints, bright peacocks, even lightning bolts. Never the same twice in a week. It became known, quietly, as the Flash Tie Protocol. A rotating spectacle meant to turn heads, distract from the substance, and signal presence without purpose. Milton didn't answer questions. He reframed them. He didn't solve problems. He redirected them. His style was smooth, his language polished, his contribution performative.

During meetings, Milton leaned back with arms crossed, letting the room orbit around him. When technical issues surfaced, he deflected with abstractions. "Let's make sure this ladders up to our strategic pillars," he would say. Or, "This feels like a great opportunity for cross-functional sponsorship." It sounded impressive. It meant nothing. Project leaders stopped asking him to remove roadblocks. Developers stopped explaining blockers. Vendors learned to speak in buzzwords only. Everyone adjusted, not because he led, but because he lingered.

Milton didn't close projects. He outlasted them. When a program reached its final phase, he had already moved on to the next photo op. When scope collapsed or deadlines slipped, he issued statements about "transitional maturity" and "ongoing optimization." But nothing landed. Nothing settled. There was no final checklist, no clean handoff, no ownership. Only a slow fade.

He was everywhere. Except where it counted. And when people looked back, there was not even the residue of work, only the echo of his voice in the minutes and an office door hook full of neckties.

Milton B. Flashover didn't fail. He evaporated. And that's what happens when closure is treated like ceremony instead of commitment. The mess doesn't end. It lingers. Until someone else shows up, with a checklist, a mop, and the will to finish strong.

No initiative he ever touched truly closed. It was declared finished in ritual, but not in substance. The cutover was incomplete. The users untrained. The inboxes full of noise, and the documents missing content. Yet there he stood, posing for the camera with his showy new necktie and a grin, while the team behind him whispered fixes into each other's ears. It was the opposite of closure. A spectacle without a system.

Based on a real person, Milton's legacy isn't unique. Where he spun spectacle, the project janitor delivers clarity. Quietly. Cleanly. Fully. Some people have the presence but not the foresight. No project, large or small, can land well without both. Presence to engage. Foresight to set the angle at inception. Now, project janitors, eyes on the path. Light the way.

The most effective way to do it, is to do it.
-- Amelia Earhart

Adding the Polish

Closure isn't just a handshake or a handoff. It's what happens next. When the room resets. When the inbox goes quiet. When no one needs to ask where the documents live, or who owns the follow-up, or what comes next. The project janitor knows this moment from the start. Arrival. When the work survives your departure. The decisions stick. You no longer hold the keys. Since day one, you have prepared to leave. That's the polish. Not the bow on top, but the scaffolding removed. The Maintenance and Operations team taking over. The path cleared from the boardroom to the launchpad. The craft exploring space. Indefinitely.

Not every closure runs smoothly. Some take your full skillset to balance what you can control - and what you can't. Then stick the landing anyway. Still, closure is about ensuring the weight of everything that came before doesn't collapse when you let go. You stood in the gaps. You cleaned what others avoided. You faced silence, scope, risk, doubt. And now, the project work is done. The new normal for your stakeholders begins. Because you finished it. Fully. The budget often decides when the project janitor walks in and how long they stay. But when the project closes, they leave with intention. They leave behind alignment. Ownership. Legacy. The checklists are signed. The mop is hung. The exit is clean. And final.

Janitor's Keyring

You see it early. You plan, act, and follow through. You make it safe to leave. You carry the lantern far enough to light the final step. Then you set it down. Closure is not the end of effort. It's the moment you can walk away, knowing the path remains. Presence withdrawn. Outcome secured - now and ongoing. Sometimes indefinitely.

The Wisdom Within: The Lantern Bearer and the Spring

There was once a trail cut long ago, marked with stones. The path was intended to lead from the village to the High Spring of Eldros, a water source so clear and cold it was said to sharpen the mind and soothe the weary. The map was drawn. The way was set. The first stones were placed with ceremony and songs. And for a time, the work continued.

But seasons passed. The council's attention turned to other plans. The workers were called elsewhere, and the path stopped short of the springs. Still, from a distance, it looked complete. The flagstones near the village stood strong. The trail had shape. But beyond the bend, the forest returned. Thorns grew. Markers fell. And in time, few remembered that the spring had ever been the goal.

Years later, when the need for water returned, the village sent travelers to find the trail again. Many tried. Most turned back early. Others looked for shortcuts. Some made it all the way to the edge of the old trail. Then, finding no water, they declared the journey finished.

But one answered the call to carry a lantern. The bearer studied the old map not just to read it, but to understand it. He started not at the trail's end where the path met the woods, but at the last stone visibly mapped. He cleared vines. Righted toppled markers. Rechecked the grade. Each step forward restored what had once been planned.

The bearer did not blaze a new trail. He revealed the one already there, hidden, intended. He worked through the quiet dusk, clearing what had grown over, setting new stones where the old had vanished, ensuring the path matched the map. He arrived. He made the end reachable again, not by carving new ways, but by completing what had been started.

There, where the water ran cold and clear, he set the final stone and placed a quiet marker. Carved not with his name, but with this: "High Spring of Eldros, the journey's end." Then he turned back. He left the spring behind him, and the trail made whole. Never again would a traveler lose their way. Some called him the Lantern Bearer. Others never knew he came. But all who walked that path after him reached the water.

That is closure. Not claimed early. Carried to completion. Remembering and achieving the goal. You do the work. You meet the objective. You close.
-- Project Janitor

Adding to Your Toolbox

Set closure as a goal from the start: Don't treat closure as an afterthought. Define what "done" means early so the entire project moves toward a shared endpoint.

Confirm readiness to finish: Before you declare victory, check what remains. Look past the dashboard. Ensure the actual work is complete, not just the status report.

Finish what others left undone: Review final deliverables, track down loose ends, and verify that what was promised has been delivered and acknowledged.

Secure operational handoff: Make sure support teams, clients, and future owners understand what to do next. Confirm documents are accessible and responsibilities are assigned.

Archive with care: Store final artifacts where they can be found. Version them. Label them clearly. Organize handoff materials with those who will need them.

Withdraw access responsibly: Remove roles and credentials no longer needed. Protect the work by ensuring it is not altered or left exposed after handoff.

Document lessons while they're fresh: Hold the retrospective. Capture what worked and what didn't. Share it forward, even if no one asks you to.

Leave the space clean: Close out the inbox. Finish the punch list. Turn out the lights. Let the next person step into clarity, not confusion.

Depart with intention: Walk the final steps. Don't drift away. Leave knowing the work holds. That is closure. That is arrival.

Chapter 18
What We Missed: The Project Janitor's Hardest Lesson

Executive Summary

Some lessons arrive with no warning. Just a cost. This chapter explores the kind of failure that can't be undone, and the role of the project janitor when a preventable risk becomes irreversible loss. Real lessons learned. Through the lens of a tragic turning point in motorsport history and the quiet wisdom of a child's learning by watching, we examine how unspoken choices become culture, how oversight becomes inheritance, and how the work of remembrance must live not in tribute alone, but in the standards built by experience. The project janitor's job isn't to mourn the moment. It's to embed the lessons, carry the memory, and make sure the next team races from a safer start.

The Mess at Hand

Some messes hold their echo. They linger. First, there's the sound, a sharp, sudden, undeniable vibration that weakens the knees. Then the silence. And then the reverberation. Not through walls, but through systems, through industries, through every corridor where voices remain: "We should have seen it." This wasn't just a risk buried in procedure. It was a caution flag, the formidable lesson that hadn't yet been realized. Ever. And when it finally was, it carried a cost no one could repay. And one the world will never forget. It arrived in a black Chevrolet Monte Carlo.

Some messes can be cleaned with a mop. Others, well, cannot be cleaned. Because when the cleanup crew arrived, there was no way to make it right. Except to change things. Difficult things. The signs had been there all along: the overlooked designs, the missed warnings, the accepted risks passed off as culture. But no one had collected them. No one had logged them. Until they couldn't ignore the message any longer. The project janitor's job wasn't to bulldoze the house. Wanted to. We all did. But no. The job was to ensure, after much renovation, it never looked that way again.

In Daytona, #3 was at hand. God's hand.

The Cleaning Strategy

There are many tools "to do." There are no tools to "undo." Sometimes, cycling the system doesn't bring it back. The project janitor knows this. What's gone is gone. What's forever broken cannot be unbroken. The job now is not to reach backward, but to steady what's ahead. You don't rewrite the moment. You mark it. You acknowledge it. And then you begin. Not with ceremony. Not with anger. Okay, a little anger. Perhaps more sadness. But always with quiet conviction. The lesson was costly. The world lost Dale. Now it must be carried. Always. And everything built from this point forward must be ready to carry it too.

The first step was to gather what had been missed. Not just one oversight or one failed design, but the pattern. Features that nearly worked. Concerns that nearly reached the right desk. Risks so common they had become background noise. A culture of near misses in a *why now*, *why him*, moment. Still, no single event caused the loss, but many contributed. The project janitor doesn't hunt for culprits. They look for the missed signs. They log what had gone unlogged, name what had gone unnamed, and begin the list that should have existed already. Because grief may not bring clarity, but damn… it demands accountability.

Sorrow is never a strategy. But it can certainly shape one. Pain becomes data. Emotion becomes input. You take what was felt and translate it into something that lasts: a design change, a process addition, a policy that doesn't flinch under pressure. In the hands of the project janitor, the pain, the lesson, doesn't stay a post-it scribble on the wall. It enters every aspect of *from now on*. The spec. The review gate. The next build. Because memorials don't prevent recurrence. Standards do.

What comes next must stand without supervision. It must protect the future without needing to reference the past. Still, we never forget. That's the mark of a true cleanup, when the system itself applies even absorbs the lesson. Not a reminder taped to a monitor, but a safety spec no one can bypass. Get it approved. Not a rule that depends on memory, but one enforced by design. Get that approved too. The project janitor doesn't build tribute. They build constraint. They change what's possible. Because what's built now has to work for people who weren't in the room when it all went wrong. You never know how many lives you might save.

Some memories are too heavy to carry alone. But if you embed them into the work, they move forward with the team. Quietly. Permanently. Not as story. As standard. Best practice. The project janitor does not pause the mission in grief. They strengthen it. They do not freeze the moment. They let it teach. And in doing so, they make room for something stronger than tribute: continuity. The work goes on. Not untouched. But changed. Better. Safer. Dear Dale. Safer. Because now, the process, the system, the team remembers. That's the strategy.

Scrub Away the Chaos

The proverbial mop doesn't move right away. Not in a mess like this. The project janitor walks in, takes one look, and knows this isn't a reset. This isn't whiteboard solvable. There's no workshop. No status update. No revised plan. No precedent. Simply a space that feels heavier than it should, and a silence that isn't accidental. The difference between a failed project and a life lost is not in the cleanup. It's in the question that follows. What now? Not how to replace. How to continue. How to walk back into the same rooms, the same track, the same seats, and do the work with eyes open. This wasn't cleanup for cleanup's sake. It was the slow, steady act of keeping the future from repeating the past.

You don't always know who's watching. That's the quiet truth behind most patterns. What we tolerate becomes culture. What we model becomes habit. And sometimes, the smallest thing we shrug off, a missed report, an ignored concern, a quiet workaround, becomes someone else's standard. That's what makes the old story worth retelling.

It began with a spoon. The grandfather's hands shook when he ate, and he spilled more than he kept. His son and daughter-in-law grew frustrated. They stopped setting a place for him at the table. They gave him a stool in the corner and a wooden bowl, so nothing would break. They thought the problem was solved. But their little boy had been watching. A few days later, he sat on the floor with scraps of wood, carving something. "What are you making?" they asked. "A trough," he said. "For you. For when you're old like Grandpa. So you won't spill." He wasn't being cruel. He was being exact. He had copied what he saw. Because that's what he thought came next. Something larger to catch the problem.

The project janitor knows that what's tolerated today gets repeated tomorrow. The lessons we teach, stick. And not always intentionally. Sometimes they're inherited. Sometimes absorbed. They can be cultural. That's why the mop matters. Not because it erases, but because it resets the standard. The reason the project janitor cleans mess after mess is because someone else will walk that path next. Someone new. Someone watching. Someone driving. And the way we leave the track says more than anything that ever happened on it. That's scrubbing the chaos. And the real hope.

Lessons from the Janitor's Closet

The hardest lessons are not always learned in the meetings we call to brainstorm them. Most are written in aftermath. Not on the whiteboard, but in strategy lost. In belts. In walls. In the shape of a cockpit. In the way a team draws the finish line and decides, "Never again," and then drives change to prove it. That's when a lesson becomes more than reflection. It becomes design. The project janitor knows that most retrospectives are filled with words. But the real ones, the ones earned, are built into next steps. Observed. Measured. They are not suggestions. They are requirements. Because if a lesson is real, it becomes the catalyst to change. Real change that holds. Even when no one's looking.

After the loss, NASCAR changed. Not only with tribute, but with infrastructure. They mandated a Head and Neck Support (HANS) device. They installed Steel and Foam Energy Reduction (SAFER) barriers at tracks. Engineers redesigned cockpits. Crews added black boxes. Officials standardized spotter communication. No single action could rewrite what happened, but together, they shaped a future where that kind of loss became far less likely. That is what the project janitor does. They take the irreparable and make it instructive. They reshape the system so the next time it holds. Not because of a speech, but because the fix is welded into the frame.

But lessons only lead a path forward if they travel. A change made in one place must inform the choices made elsewhere. That's why project janitors study the moments that count, not to dwell, but to distribute. They take the fix, the insight, the hindsight, whatever it is, and ensure it reaches the next project, the next build, the next team. That is how standards evolve. Not by accident. By attention. Because if the lesson only lives in the place it was learned, then it risks dying there too. In the end, success is found in the lessons learned and the path next taken.

Every lesson worth keeping must survive the handoff. That's the test. Not whether a team learns something once, but whether the next team starts from that revised knowledge. Project janitors don't just document.

They transmit. They don't just fix. They teach how not to need the fix again. What was once an echo now becomes a framework. A brace. A boundary. A foundation. Something that doesn't just remember what happened but prevents it from happening again. That's the quiet legacy of the project janitor. Not just the lesson. Proof that the lesson was learned and the changes adopted.

Spills and Cleanup

Some spills begin with what wasn't decided. The risk that sat unnoticed or worse ignored. That detail everyone assumed someone else had handled. The cleanup didn't start with action. It started with a reckoning. A slow, structured facing of what had been overlooked because it felt familiar. That's where real change begins. Not with what went wrong, but with what was never questioned.

The list was long. And overdue. Risks long tolerated. Designs too long unchanged. Safety features shelved in favor of speed, familiarity, or cost. Each item on the cleanup list wasn't a discovery. It was an admission. They had been there. All of them. Just waiting for the right eyes. The right polish. The project janitor knows that the hardest cleanups are made of things people already knew but didn't act on. Until they had to.

To their credit, some saw it coming. The data existed. The tools were known. Quiet efforts had already begun to evaluate new standards, new devices, new designs long before the tragedy. But the urgency wasn't shared. The push wasn't unified. And when there is no clear mandate, momentum dies in the margins. That's why the cleanup mattered. Not to shame the past, but to galvanize the future. Not to say, "we never cared," but to prove we would never again wait to care this much.

Not every risk is a lesson. A lesson often strikes only when the risk is realized. And once it does, all that matters now is what you do next.
-- Project Janitor

Adding the Polish

Cleanups always come too late to prevent the moment that called for the mop. But the polish still matters. Because polish does not repair. It preserves. It shows that the work now remembers. That the culture, the system, the legacy retains what memory alone cannot. When recording the lesson, the project janitor does not dwell on the tragedy. They reinforce the learning. Confirm the restraint. Review and revise the spec with appropriate diligence to ensure the lessons endure. Because someone is watching from the stands, hoping to follow.

The project janitor doesn't just speak the lesson. They walk it. It's in the checklist reviewed after the rush has cleared. The bolt checked that never fails. The harness cinched for the driver who never asked. These aren't precautions. They're memory in motion. The kind that doesn't continually replay the loss and yet never forgets it. That's the polish. Not the shell's shine for looks. Just the quiet, practiced performance of doing things right. Holding the light. Clearing the trail. Because the lesson's not written on the wall. It's built into the work. And everyone else is learning by watching.

Janitor's Keyring

Some lessons leave no second chance. The project janitor doesn't wait for another warning. From the moment they arrive, they record what's learned. They carry the memory forward through the work itself. Not only as tribute, but as traction. So the next generation can race from there.

The Wisdom Within: The Old Grandfather and His Grandson

It began with a spoon.

The old man's hands had grown uncertain. Every meal, they trembled. Soup spilled. Bread dropped. Utensils clinked to the floor and stayed there. At first, the family offered kindness. But kindness eroded into discomfort, and discomfort hardened into convenience.

They stopped setting a place for him at the table. Gave him a stool near the hearth instead. Served him from a wooden bowl, so nothing could spill or break. The conversation moved on without him.

He did not complain.

But someone else had been watching.

The boy, no more than five, studied the changes. He saw the silence. The separation. He saw the wooden bowl and the bent shoulders behind it. And though no one explained the change, he saw its pattern.

A few days later, the boy gathered scraps of wood. Sat cross-legged on the floor, carving with a dull tool and deep intent. His parents found him focused, hands steady in a way they hadn't noticed before.

"What are you making?" they asked.

He looked up, calm.

"A trough," he said. "For you. For when you're old like Grandpa. So you won't spill."

He wasn't being cruel. He wasn't joking.

He was following the plan.

He had copied what he saw. Not the words. Not the frustration. Just the solution. The accommodation. The consequence of someone no longer fitting the frame. He thought it was his turn to prepare the next one.

Because when people stop explaining, habits become instructions. And when systems tolerate exclusion, they teach it.

The lesson was clear. Not because it had been taught. Because it had been witnessed.

The man and his wife looked at each other for a while, and then they began to cry. Then they took the old grandfather to the table, and thereafter always let him eat with them at the table. And they stayed silent through every spill.

-- Brothers Grimm, as told by a Project Janitor

Adding to Your Toolbox

Recognize the cost: Understand that the impact is real and irreversible. Let the gravity of what happened shape how seriously the next steps are taken.

Study the failure: Examine what contributed. Not just one oversight, but the entire pattern. Look for missed warnings, ignored risks, and signs that were normalized.

Collect what was overlooked: Identify concerns that were never logged, risks dismissed as routine, and decisions that quietly allowed danger to persist.

Document the truth: Record what should have been noted all along. Not just the incident, but the culture that tolerated it. Turn the silence into specifics.

Transform grief into standards: Use the emotion of the moment to drive permanent change. Design the lesson into systems, checklists, reviews, and rules.

Embed the fix into the work: Adjust specifications and processes so they reflect what was learned. Make sure the safeguards exist whether memory does or not.

Repeat until normal: Let the correction become routine. Make it part of inspections, reviews, and peer checks until no one questions its presence.

Pass it forward: Share what was learned across teams and projects. Ensure the next group begins from a stronger position, not the same vulnerable one.

Model the lesson daily: Show the standard in every action. Let the quiet consistency of your behavior teach what the event made clear.

Design for those not in the room: Build systems that protect people who did not witness the loss. Let your work prevent what memory alone cannot.

Chapter 19
The Janitor's Inspection: Holding the Line After the Calm

Executive Summary

This chapter is not about ending the work. It is about staying with it, after the launch, after the handoff, when attention fades and the real risks begin to emerge. Calm is not confirmation. Progress is not alignment. And trust is not truth unless it is checked. Project janitors know this. They return to inspect what looks finished. They scrub not for shine, but to reveal what is buried, missed.

Through the story of AI's rise, from quiet research to global deployment, we examine how the absence of visible chaos can hide deeper misalignments. As the systems scaled, so did the silence. And into that silence stepped a new kind of steward. One who would catch what slipped, ensuring what is built can stand.

In this final act, we reaffirm the role. Not as maintainer, but as last witness. The one who polishes for more than appearance, for integrity. The one who maintains the heading when no one else remembers to check the stars. Because the work does not end when it ships. It ends when it holds. And that only happens if someone stays long enough to make sure it is right.

The Mess at Hand

Modern messes are growing harder to notice. The stains are still present. Everywhere. But now they manifest through automation, abstraction, and unchecked speed, much of it driven by AI. The problem isn't that projects are breaking more often. It's that when they do, it's harder to tell. In every field, in every role, work has grown faster, quieter, more complex. The signs are subtle now. The missed inspection. The system trained on the wrong inputs. The auto-response that flips a switch without telling anyone it had. This is the new mess. Not scattered like debris but settled like dust. Still real. Still expanding.

The tools have evolved dramatically in the last decade. Smart factories, 3D printing, AI schedulers, predictive dashboards. Every field now runs on something faster than human pace. From cloud platforms to embedded systems, the work moves with speed and accuracy. But that doesn't mean the project keeps stride.

No matter how much the tools advance, people still behave like people. They miss things. They let assumptions ride too long. They push effort to the side because it isn't their milestone, never mind that it's someone else's critical path. Some delays show up in metrics. Others hide in habits. Avoided conversations. Unclear accountability. Work that keeps moving, but not always in the right direction. The mess at hand remains in no danger of extinction. And for as long as it takes, a project janitor will be there to help make things right.

When projects fall, they don't collapse all at once. They wear down the people managing them. Routine, relentless issues. Clients who change direction. Vendors who miss deadlines. Dependencies that move faster than clarity. The project team does their best, yet watches the plan slide sideways. Then comes the call. Enter the project janitor. Not a savior. Just someone with a fresh voice and a full toolbox. And here's the part no one says out loud: they face the same relentless challenges. The same mess. The same pressure. What changes is how they hold the line. How they keep the project, and themselves, from unraveling. Then they deliver. Then they clean up. Then they rest. And then, without fanfare, they take on the next one. For a career. Stress hits hard for the first five years. Ten. Twenty. Forty. Truth? It doesn't get easier. It just gets deeper. More human. More brutal. More real. Still, vastly rewarding.

This is the mess at hand. Not just spilled coffee or missed deadlines, but systems stretched thin, people under pressure, and patterns that quietly repeat until someone draws the line and holds it. It's the grain of sand in your shoe. It doesn't matter if the project is high-tech or hand-built. The pressure feels the same. The quiet tension builds the same. And when no one else steps in to identify it, the mess keeps moving. Unless someone does something. Unless someone steps forward. That's where the work begins. And that's the role of the project janitor.

PLAYBOOK FOR PROJECT JANITORS

The Cleaning Strategy

The project janitor walks in with a strategy, not a solution. They find their footing. Observe and pause. Not to delay the work, but to brace it. Every handoff comes with turbulence. Tools applied too early. Sequencing disrupted. People stretched too thin. Decisions made before understanding their consequences. The first job is to stabilize. Not the plan, yet. Not the team, yet. Themselves. Because when pressure spikes and expectations tilt, presence becomes the anchor. That's how the role survives. Not by promising a miracle, but by modeling what steadiness looks like in the middle of the mess. Stoic. True.

With their footing sustained, the project janitor begins to assess. Not by untangling everything at once, but by scanning for what the rush overlooked. AI and automation systems report what they see. Dashboards confirm what they're told. But something still feels off. A delay with no root cause. A decision that didn't land. A team that keeps delivering on time, but never full scope. That's where the project janitor focuses, not on what the system shows, but on what it quietly resists. The cleanup doesn't begin with explanation. It begins with pattern awareness, sourcing emotional friction, and asking questions no tool knows how to ask. That's what keeps the role alive. Not brilliance. Not blame. Simply a sharper kind of listening.

The strategy is clean. The project janitor doesn't carry it all alone. They rely on the team, the tools, and the process. They review the outputs, apply the lessons for future inputs, and use feedback to guide them. Over time, they learn when to rest, when to delegate, when to trust the tool, but still check the result. They know how to spot good help and how to receive it. Other hands appear. People step in, not necessarily to fix, but to follow. AI helps too, not by replacing judgment, but by catching what's easy to miss when fatigue sets in. The system gets stronger. The work gets lighter. Not because the mess is gone, but because the project janitor isn't walking through it alone anymore.

The project janitor doesn't reject the tools. They use them. But always with context. AI can highlight patterns, flag anomalies, and cluster defects, but it can't feel when urgency is real or when a milestone only looks met. No intuition. That judgment still lives in the room. In the pauses between updates. In the hesitation behind someone's "we're good." The project janitor pays attention to what the tool doesn't measure: fatigue, uncertainty, distance. They're not fighting modern systems. They're anchoring them. Keeping automation from drifting into assumption. That's how the role endures. Not as resistance to change, but as the bearing wall that supports it.

Cracks don't always form in crisis. More often, they slip in during the quiet. When the chaos fades and momentum feels restored, that's when the checklist gets skipped. The confirmation email goes unsent. The tension that once made the team precise is gone, and with it, their edge. The project janitor watches for that moment. Because the riskiest period isn't always the storm. It's the silence that follows. Once stability is in force and the day-to-day work of delivery resumes, it's easy to believe the job is done. But that's where a quiet ebb turns into drift. The project janitor doesn't just clean up until the turmoil passes. They build habits strong enough to hold through fair seas. That's what keeps the project, and the role, from fading back into assumption. Many ships are lost under clear skies.

Scrub Away the Chaos

When calm arrives, chaos hasn't vanished. It's an undercurrent in waiting. You don't feel the pull at first. But if no one checks the heading, drift begins. Scrubbing is no longer surface work. Not here. It's not for shine. It's to expose the unrest beneath the stillness. After the crisis quiets and the dashboard dims, what's left behind isn't peace, it's sediment. Layered decisions. Half-tracked risks. Assumptions hardened over time. Things too small for the ticket queue, too quiet to escalate, but too risky to leave alone. This is the mess that remains after the mess. And this is where the project janitor returns, not with polish, but to take ownership. To wipe away what clouds the next step. To reveal what's still breathing underneath.

The project janitor doesn't announce the scrub. They begin it. Quietly. A reopened task. A question about data no one remembers entering. A meeting recap sent with the details no one wanted to hear. The work is deliberate. Clearing the lens. Stopping the spread of unowned assumptions. Tracing where direction softened, where habit replaced heading, where the wheel was left untouched because the waters looked still. Scrubbing starts with the smallest correction. A sentence reworded. A risk revisited. A false "Done" reopened before the wind returns. The wind will return.

Lessons from the Janitor's Closet

Artificial Intelligence (AI) didn't arrive with a lightning bolt. It emerged like any large system, piece by piece, white paper by white paper. Too slow to warn. Too complex to stop. Too abstract to clean as it grew. No charter. No sponsor. Merely a momentum made of models, academic papers, and good intentions. That's how big messes emerge from the deep. Quiet, stable. And when they surface, they don't resemble chaos. They look like something already well built. But is it? Paint on patches. Plaster over horsehair. Somewhere in there, you'll find a house. Built not from a plan, but from the accumulation of untested parts and unchecked progress. Open source. And while headlines framed AI as a breakthrough, those watching from within saw something more familiar. A project with no owner. A backlog with no grooming. A stack of tools deployed faster than anyone could confirm the foundation beneath them.

The Giant was born in fragments. Research papers. Training sets. Quiet grants. There was no declaration of purpose. No final requirements. No architect sketching the whole. No standard. Just early teams nudging the edges of possibility. The wild west. Fun times. Academic labs. Research collectives. Open-source contributors. Each laying down a line of code or a line of theory without seeing the structure take shape. Neural networks. Symbolic logic. Early speech recognition. All working in silos, failing often, but sharing what they learned. Not because they knew where it was going. But because that's what explorers do. They leave trails of breadcrumbs, hoping someone eventually finds a path. And that they did.

AI did not appear through a single invention, but a convergence. Between 2017 and 2020, transformer models changed the scale of what was possible. Digital engines such as GPT, BERT, and T5 became capable of summarizing, translating, and generating human-like language. These models moved AI from research into something tangible and usable. What had once been academic figments became usable. Research labs turned into startups. Models evolved into platforms. OpenAI released GPT-2, then 3, then 4 each unleashing progressively more capability. Google expanded its language tools. Meta developed LLaMA. Microsoft made its move. Cohere and MiniMax joined the race. What began as exploration had become a global pursuit. The code was moving faster than the questions could be answered.

With acceleration came abstraction. System interfaces made it easy. Prompts replaced programming. Layers of Application Programming Interfaces (APIs) and integrations masked the underlying model. Users no longer needed to understand how it worked. They just needed to ask and click. And for a while, it all worked, perhaps too well. The tools became readily available. Dirt cheap. The platforms grew. Everything looked calm. But underneath that calm, something was surfacing. No one was checking the sails. No one was confirming the source data or questioning what had been embedded along the way. The lack of trouble tickets wasn't proof of stability but a sign of the quiet turn. No one was watching closely enough.

Then came the inspections. Not to slow progress, but to understand what had already been shipped. Red Teamers. Alignment teams. Safety reviewers. Policy analysts. They weren't brought in to build. They were brought in to check the math. To follow the trail of unexamined assumptions. To question defaults that had hardened into features. Their job was to find out whether AI would remain viable. Project janitors, all. Quiet. Methodical. Necessary. Because by the time the sails are flapping, it may be too late to check the heading.

What they found wasn't failure but friction. Plenty of it. Misalignments layered into design. Incentives coded into outcomes. Hallucinations dismissed as edge cases. Biased data recycled as standard input. Behaviors shaped by what the models were trained to reinforce, and no one retrained them. No single point of collapse. Just quiet accumulations. Skipped reviews. Missing audit trails. Metrics optimized without understanding what they were rewarding. Decisions made at speed, now hardened into infrastructure. This wasn't a system on fire. It was a system meandering without a compass. And the deeper they looked, the clearer it became. The problem wasn't capability. It was consequence. No one had asked what might happen if it all worked. And it worked. Now what?

Cleanup started quietly. Red teams grew challenging systems, assumptions, and defenses. Teams added audit trails after launch, trying to retrofit accountability into systems that had already gone live. Engineers added safety systems to models that had already shipped. Tech companies rolled out alignment updates, content filters, usage dashboards, and escalation paths. But cleanup at scale requires more than policy. It requires project janitors. Pattern recognition. And many patterns still escaped scrutiny. AI hallucinations continued. Disinformation risks multiplied. Human labor stayed hidden behind automation. Some platforms added checks. Others chased market share. The mess hid in plain sight but many still failed to see it. Fixing the surface doesn't restore the structure. Not without someone watching the foundation.

Today, AI is everywhere. But so is the need to check the heading. The project janitor watches for storms. Not to run from them, but to be sure the ship is ready. To check what others assume. To hold the line when calm masks the risk. The next advancement won't be defined by what we build. It will be defined by what we keep upright when the wind returns. Because it's not enough that the system continues to move.

Someone still has to make sure it's moving in the right direction. The lesson? Ready the ship.

Spills and Cleanup

The true trial of readiness begins after the launch. When the dashboards turn green, the hands pull back, and the press release fades, that's when the real test begins. Systems rarely fail in a burst. They veer, especially when no one stays at the wheel. The illusion of calm is what catches teams off guard. The assumption that movement equals progress. That an empty inbox means all is well. But project janitors know better. A clean handoff doesn't guarantee a clear course. Even a ship that sails straight can find itself adrift if the current goes unmeasured.

The risks that matter aren't always dramatic. It's not the flood that breaks the system. It's the slow leak no one charted. A mislabeled record. A stale assumption. A decision made under pressure that never got revisited. Left alone, these don't cause collapse. They cause fatigue. Teams spend their energy cleaning up the same problems, rerouting the same errors, explaining the same confusion to new users. The system keeps moving, but it doesn't improve. Progress gets buried under workaround. And by the time someone notices, the source is hard to trace.

It isn't the storm that wears you out but the stillness after the winds have passed knowing the next one is on the way.
-- Project Janitor

Adding the Polish

This wasn't touch-up work. This was the inspection of a living system already in use, already embedded, already trusted by people who don't know what it took to build it, or what's hiding inside. The polish at this scale isn't about formatting or finesse. It's about integrity. It's the catch before the consequence. The field left blank that powers a decision. The setting carried forward from a test environment. The false default still influencing results. At this point, polish isn't about making it better. It's about making sure what's here can be trusted. For good.

Because the handoff matters. The project janitor doesn't walk away with information stashed in their pocket. They surface everything the maintenance and operations team, the homeowner, or the next steward needs. They document it. They say it out loud. No riddles. No mysteries. No withheld detail that could cause the next person to stumble. That's the ethic. That's the role. The cleanup isn't done until someone else can walk in and stand steady.

The project janitor doesn't linger. They stay until the job is finished, until the system can stand on its own, without excuse. Adding the polish is the last measure of respect. A number double-checked because it anchors more than one report. A sentence rewritten so it means what it says, not just what it hopes. A step removed from the process because it solves a problem that no longer exists. These aren't enhancements. They are decisions. Final ones. Quiet corrections that leave behind stability. When they walk away, there's nothing left to untangle. Nothing hidden. Just a system ready to be used by people who may never know who made it work, who made it safe, who did it right.

That's the work. The role to keep alive. Not to be seen, but to be counted on. Not to take credit, but to take care. Some will inherit what was built. Others will expand it. But someone had to stabilize it first. Someone had to stand still while the rest moved on, just long enough to be sure it would stand. That's the job. That's the final polish.

Janitor's Keyring

Mr. Planwell never rushed. He walked the hall with keys at his side, sometimes jangling, always present. Not every door was his to open. But if one jammed, he was the one they called. Most of the keys didn't have labels. Some were for rooms no one used anymore. Some had been copied so many times they barely fit. A few were bent, but they still worked, because he knew how to turn them. That's experience.

The project janitor carries a keyring of their own. Not of metal, but of memory. A quiet set of lessons. An ever-growing toolbox, not made for ceremony, but for real work. Not every key fits. Some are for things left locked too long. Some were never supposed to be used again. Lessons missed. But the ring stays full, because the work keeps showing up. You don't need every key. You need the right one at the right time. Perhaps to open what no one else wants to touch. To lock what others keep leaving ajar.

That's what the keyring is for. Not to show authority, but to carry responsibility. And often, accountability. To remember what was fixed. To return when it sticks again. To hand off the right key, not keep it in your pocket. Because someone else needs to open the same door without guessing.

The longer you do this work, the more you'll recognize the pattern. It's never just the key. It's knowing when and how to use it. So, hang it up when you're done. Leave it somewhere someone else will find it. And when they do, they'll know. Someone came before. Someone stayed late. Someone left the place clean.

And before you shut off the lights and lock the door, give someone else a chance to take their first swing.

The Wisdom Within: The Sailor and the Stillness

There was once a captain of quiet reputation. He had no medals, no lineage, and no shipyard bore his name. But every sailor in the old waters knew his vessel had never floundered. He was not the loudest, nor the fastest. But when storms blackened the sky and the sea turned on its own, it was said the captain grew calm. He did not raise his voice. He did not question the wave. He simply worked, and others followed. He knew how to steer by stars even when they were hidden.

His crew was young, many on their first long voyage. They were proud to sail with a man like him, though few understood why he never smiled when the weather was fair.

After crossing a stretch of contested current, the ship passed into waters where the wind fell away. The sails drooped. The waves flattened. For days, the sea made no sound. The men called it mercy. They polished the rails. They played games on the deck. They stopped logging the course. A task was missed, but it seemed small. A bearing went unchecked, but the sea did not speak. No alarms sounded. And so, slowly, the crew came to believe the silence meant safety.

The captain, ever the sailor, walked the deck each night to listen. All was calm. He did not speak. A quiet sea can test conviction better than a storm. He did not wake the crew or reset the heading. Some truths, he knew, only take root in stillness.

And then, without warning, the wind returned. It struck from the side. The sails caught and stretched. The ship leapt in an unexpected direction. The compass no longer aligned. The stars whispered a different route. They had not held their heading. They had not held their line.

The crew scrambled to adjust, but the sea does not forgive delay.

When they finally reached land, a young helmsman asked the captain, "Was it the wind that turned us wrong?"

The captain looked once at the sail, once at the sea, and then back at the crew.

"No," he said. "It wasn't the wind. It was the stillness. In a storm, no man forgets to steer."

And that was all.

But in every harbor they reached afterward, the crew retold the tale. Not of the storm. Not of the wind. But of the days the sea grew quiet, and how they learned what calmness can steal. They told how a ship could drift if not from injury, but from indifference. How a heading can slip without sound. And how even the sturdiest vessel will veer, if no one takes the wheel.

And they told it often. Because many ships are lost not when the sails are full, but when they hang in stillness and no one checks the stars.

Check the closet, check the list, check the stars.
-- Project Janitor

Adding to Your Toolbox

Reenter after calm: Do not assume that stability means success. Return to the work once the launch is complete and verify what others may have stopped watching.

Ground yourself first: Before you assess the project, stabilize yourself. Presence under pressure becomes the anchor others rely on.

Inspect the invisible: Look beyond the dashboards. Watch for subtle signals that the system is drifting. A missed confirmation. A vague update. A habit that replaced alignment.

Use the tools, but check the result: Let automation assist you, but do not depend on it blindly. Review outputs with context and question what feels off.

Follow the friction: Pay attention to hesitation, confusion, and unresolved issues that remain after go-live. These are indicators of deeper misalignment.

Reopen what was assumed closed: Surface tasks, risks, or issues that were prematurely marked complete. If it was rushed or assumed, it must be reverified.

Expose quiet drift: Trace where accountability has softened. Where assumptions replaced confirmation. Address direction before the gap widens.

Surface what the next team needs: Do not hold on to knowledge. Make it accessible. Say it out loud. Document clearly. Confirm someone can carry it.

Finish with integrity: Correct the small things. The number that anchors a report. The sentence that needs to be clear. The step that no longer adds value.

Hand off with confidence: Leave no mystery. Ensure what remains is not only functional but understood. Walk away knowing it will stand.

~

Join us at:
ProjectJanitors.com

Author's Epilog
The Project Janitor's Final Sweep

Forty years. That's how long I have walked the corridors of project delivery. Some clean, some cluttered, some still echoing with the noise of the last meeting. I didn't always carry a mop. I didn't always know the name of the role. But from the earliest days with Mr. Planwell - keys on his hip, wisdom in his step - I began to understand what the work really was. It wasn't leadership by title. It was service by conviction. It was caring when others moved on. It was staying when the crowd had left. It was cleaning up, yes. But more than that, it was carrying forward.

This book was written not just as a record, but as a thank-you. To those who taught me. To those who handed me the broom. And now, to you, the one still holding it.

You stayed to the end. That matters to me. Because I know what that takes. I know what it costs to see something through when the glamour fades and the real weight sets in. And I know the reward that waits on the other side. No applause. No headline. But something quieter. Something better. The moment when you know that what you leave behind will stand long after you say goodbye.

That's the reward. That's the polish.

If there is one thing I can pass to you, it is this: You are allowed to care. Deeply. Quietly. Without credit. You are allowed to lead by listening, to serve by steadying, to make the work cleaner, not just by fixing the mess, but by preventing it. You are allowed to be the one who inspects what others rush, who asks what others assume, who shows up not for glory, but because it's right.

You are allowed to be a Project Janitor.

And if you take up that work, if you choose to see the value in what others overlook, to build trust where others chase attention, to hold your heading even when the wind goes against you - then I promise, the role will give back. In clarity. In conviction. In the quiet pride of a job done completely.

This is not the end of your reading. It's the beginning of your stewardship. The mop is yours now. So is the keyring. And the toolbox. Add to it. Use it. Pass it forward. Leave something behind that lasts.

With gratitude deeper than these words can hold,

Thank you.
-- A fellow Project Janitor, D. Ciarcia Jr.

If you've found this book useful, please consider leaving a review.

www.ingramcontent.com/pod-product-compliance
Lightning Source LLC
Chambersburg PA
CBHW050635160426
43194CB00010B/1678